Haunted Dorset

By Chris Ellis & Andy Owens

S. B. Publications

First published in 2004 by S. B. Publications
19 Grove Road, Seaford, East Sussex BN25 1TP

ISBN 1-85770-291-3

Designed and Typeset by EH Graphics (01273) 515527

Printed by Fotolito Longo, Bolzano, Italy

Contents

Foreword by Tom Perrott 8

Introduction by the authors 9

BEAMINSTER 11

The ghost of John Daniel haunts St Mary's Church. In life, John had suffered from fits and it was these that were thought to be the cause of his death when his body was discovered a short distance from his mother's home. After his school friends had reported seeing his ghost on several occasions, a local magistrate had his body disinterred and discovered that the boy had in fact been strangled. Also in Beaminster is a modern ASSAP investigation into a haunting at Bell Farm

BLANDFORD 13

A mixture of tales from Blandford. A letter from a local lady, who prefers to remain anonymous, tells of the haunting of a dis-used railway near the River Stour. Also a haunting at Blandford Army Camp.

BOURNEMOUTH 15

An assortment of ghosts with original letters from John D. Tuffin & Gill Wilson.

BOVINGTON CAMP 20

Clouds Hill/Gallows Hill.
This is the haunting ground of Lawrence of Arabia, where the throaty sound of his Brough motorcycle has been heard in the vicinity of the cottage. Like Drake, Lawrence's ghost is said to return whenever Britain is in danger. Incorporates an original letter from Cliff Rogers, concerning Gallows Hill.

BRIDPORT 26

A range of modern reports from The Bull Hotel, The Art Gallery and Museum, The Bridport Arms Hotel and Broomhill Farmhouse. Also, an original letter from Marie Metu concerning Gypsy Lane.

BROWNSEA ISLAND 30

Recounting the experiences of Angela Morris, a local of Brownsea Island.

CORFE CASTLE 31

The setting for many strange events. In AD 978, King Edward the Martyr was murdered at Corfe Castle and later King John starved to death twenty-two French noblemen. In recent times, locals have seen the ghost of a headless woman on the pathway leading to the castle.

CREEKMOOR 34

A letter to the authors from a Miss White telling of a haunting at the park at Millfield, near Creekmoor.

DEWLISH 35

Betsey Caine's Corner.
Letter from Edward Parsons.

DORCHESTER 36

Athelhampton House
Athelhampton House stands on the banks of the River Piddle, on the site where the palace of the legendary King Athelstan once stood. This house has a myriad of secret passageways and priest holes running through it and is haunted by at least seven ghosts, all of which appear to be friendly. A 'grey lady', a 'hooded monk' and a 'spectral ape' are among the ghosts at this prolific haunted site.

DORCHESTER 40

Wolfeton House.
The ghost of Thomas Trenchard has been heard driving his ghostly coach-and-four up the main staircase of the house. Wolfeton also has a 'grey lady' and the ghost of a sad girl who had married into the household.

EGGARDON HILL 42

Eggardon Hill.
Powerstock Village.
The phantoms of Powerstock village.

HOLT, NEAR WIMBORNE 43

A letter from Mrs Snell who saw three ghosts in a cottage - but her husband and the two cottage owners did not believe her!

LYME REGIS 44

Bettiscombe Manor.
Bettiscombe House, near Lyme Regis, is better known as 'the house of the screaming skull'. Strange manifestations have occurred here whenever the ageing skull is removed from the house. Also, the haunting of the Royal Lion Hotel in Broad Street.
Lychett Matravers.

MELBURY OSMOND 48

The ghost of the Rest and Welcome Inn.

NORTH ALLINGTON **49**

The Boot Inn.
The haunting of the Boot Inn at North Allington.

POOLE **50**

A range of hauntings from a shop in Poole High Street to the Crown Hotel, Byngley House, the Guildhall Museum and the United Reformed Church.

SANDFORD ORCAS **55**

Sandford Orcas Manor.
One of the most haunted houses in Britain, with sightings right up to modern times. Sandford Orcas has as many as fourteen ghosts haunting its Tudor rooms.

SHAFTESBURY ABBEY **61**

The ghost of a monk who buried his treasure in the ruins of the Abbey can still be seen today. Reports of the monk walking as if cut off at the knees are among the many sightings.
The Grosvenor Hotel, Shaftesbury.

SHERBORNE **64**

Sherborne Castle.
Previous owners include the Earl of Somerset and Sir Walter Raleigh, both of whom were executed. The ghost of Sir Walter has been seen on many occasions, while in more recent times other apparitions have been seen.

SIXPENNY HANDLEY **66**

The phantom horseman of Sixpenny Handley. An article written by Robert Snow's grandfather.

TARRANT GUNVILLE **69**

Eastbury Park.
On certain nights of the year a coach driven by a headless horseman is said to drive from Eastbury and return, carrying William Doggett to the house where he alights and proceeds to the same panelled room where he shot himself all those years earlier. A single shot can be heard and then silence.

THORNCOMBE **71**

Forde Abbey.
Once a Cistercian Abbey, but now a prominent private house, the ghost of a monk in black can be seen walking in what would have been the cloisters. Could this be the ghost of Thomas Chard?

TYNEHAM 73

A press report of a haunting from Tyneham.

WAREHAM 74

The strange sighting of a doppelganger by a delivery driver.

WEST ALLINGTON 75

The Plymouth Inn.
Strange goings-on at The Plymouth Inn.

WEYMOUTH 76

An original letter from Jacqueline Whayman-Pover.

WIMBORNE 77

The haunting of the Barley Mow pub at Broom Hill.

APPENDIX I 78

'A CHILLING TASK'
Interviews with Dorset ghost researchers Tom Perrott and Robert Snow.

APPENDIX II 84

'SHADOWS AT MY SIDE'
Interviews with Dorset mediums Olga Bamforth and Royston Breeze.

Dedication

From Chris Ellis: My wife Julie and children Jodie, Connor and Brandon; Grandma Ellis; Karen, Rob, Kelly & Kirsty Holden; Eddie and Cynthia Rimmer; Jackie, Karl, Heather & Ryan Trevelyan; Scott, Carla, Kane & Elaisha Davidson; Grandad Ellis.

From Andy Owens: For my best mates Silvia Haller and Anne E. Knight.

Acknowledgements

The authors would like to thank everyone who assisted in their research, including Mrs Jane Macleod, senior librarian at Weymouth Library; Miss P. E. Parker, MCLIP, local studies officer at Poole Local History Centre; Ms Jane Read, senior librarian at Bridport Library; the many newspaper editors and staff who helped publicise our appeal for original experiences, the staff of Dorset tourist information centres for answering our questions, and the many people mentioned within these pages who replied to us.

Special thanks to mediums Olga Bamforth and Royston Breeze; psychic researchers Tom Perrott and Robert Snow. Particular thanks to Tom for many years of friendship to Andy Owens and for writing a wonderful Foreword for their book.

Foreword

Although I emigrated from Dorset, the county of my birth, many years ago, I have always retained a deep affection for the area that has remained so close to my heart over such a long period of time.

It is therefore with very great pleasure that I have been honoured by being asked to write a foreword to a book which I hope will familiarise many people with this area which, over the centuries, has preserved many visible and tangible traces of its ancient history. It has given birth to such eminent men of letters as Thomas Hardy and William Barnes, but at the same time has managed to keep itself enveloped in an atmosphere of mystery and legend.

All sorts of inexplicable phenomena are alleged to have manifested themselves over the years, the keys to which have still to be discovered. The solemn marching of a Roman legion across Flowers Barrow and the sound of a Brough Superior motorcycle ridden by Lawrence of Arabia on his last fateful journey from Clouds Hill, have served to link the present time with many strange happenings alleged to have taken place during the centuries before.

I commend this book to all its readers, partly from a natural pride in the county of my birth, but also as a region of which, to many of them, may be an undiscovered land of enigma and romance.

TOM PERROTT

The Society of Dorset Men and former
Chairman of The Ghost Club (founded 1862)

Introduction

It has been estimated that one-in-ten of us will see a ghost in our lifetime. Could that one-in-ten be you?

Browse through any volume on ghosts and you will no doubt discover that Dorset ranks highly as one of the most haunted counties in Britain.

But is this so surprising?

In a county which has borne witness to battle and bloodshed, poverty and disease, murder and treachery, love and romance, it seems fitting that Dorset has retained permanent phantom traces of our ancestors who have lived, worked, fought and died here.

Neither author of this book can claim any county connections, so it has been an even greater journey of discovery for us.

Like the spooks of Dorset, we also haunted its towns and villages in the course of our research. We have combed library and newspaper archives, interviewed local people who kindly recounted their personal experiences, and chatted to the owners, tenants and curators of some of the better-known haunted properties.

Delving into the history of this fascinating county, we sought out castles, ruins and stately residencies, buried deep in the Dorset countryside, reached down the narrowest of winding, leafy lanes - and regularly getting lost in the process (!) - in our quest for the quaint, the creepy and the curious.

And we have never once wondered whether to cut a story from this collection, worried it may clutter our manuscript, thus proving that the varied ghosts of Dorset may at times appear to be eccentric, bizarre, violent, tragic, frightening, comical - but never dull.

It is a sobering thought that in a world dominated by technology and apparent universal knowledge, there still appear to be areas of human experience, which remain untapped and unclassified, along the uncertain line between fact and fantasy, where even the mighty scientists fear to tread.

'Haunted Dorset' is a chance to take a step out of the hustle and bustle of this busy, self-assured world, to explore the darkened corridors, cobwebbed attics and spooky stairwells within the walls of these creepy castles and haunted houses.

Spare a moment to stand alone and in silence, breathing in the past - and maybe, just maybe, you will catch a brief glimpse of a scene long forgotten; an errant knight in search of adventure and glory, a ghostly grey lady gliding effortlessly down a corridor, or a phantom monk knelt in silent prayer.

We hope the readers of this volume enjoy reading this book as much as we have enjoyed compiling it.

And if any of you have seen a ghost - perhaps even rubbed shoulders with an apparition featured within these pages - then drop us a line, c/o our publishers, as we would love to hear from you.

In the meantime, good ghost-hunting!

CHRIS ELLIS & ANDY OWENS

Yorkshire
April 2004

Beaminster

ST MARY'S CHURCH

In 1728, the body of John Daniel was found in a field near to his home in Beaminster. As he was known to have suffered from fits throughout his short life, his death was declared as down to natural causes.

However, later that year, five local boys, four of whom had known John - one of them was his half-brother - reported seeing his ghost, holding a pen, a book and sitting near a coffin in the school room which was then located inside St Mary's Church.

As soon as one of the boys threw a stone at the apparition, John's ghost, the pen, the book and the coffin all disappeared.

St. Mary's Church, Beaminster.

Questioned by a local magistrate, he was amazed to find that all of the boys' accounts tallied and he decided to exhume John's grave. On examining his body, it was discovered that John Daniel had been the victim of strangulation.

Although no one was brought to justice for the crime, it seems that John's ghost was never seen again. A curious postscript to the haunting appears below under the entry on 'Bell Farm'.

BELL FARM

A local farmer, David Potter, reported seeing two ghosts on his property at Bell Farm. The report appeared in The Bridport News on 27th August 1998, and in September he was visited by two investigators for the research group ASSAP (the Association for the Scientific Study of Anomalous Phenomena), of which co-author Andy Owens has been a member for several years.

Stephen Hall and Ian Percy asked Mr Potter to recount what he had experienced on the 18th August 1998.

At 4.45am, Mr Potter went out into the field, which is adjacent to the burial site of John Daniel (the murdered boy in the previous entry), to check on the welfare of his cows as they were calving at this time. As he approached one of the cows he saw two figures standing over the animal as if watching it.

Although his torch was not switched on, the farmer clearly saw the two people. One was a woman dressed in a long, white flowing garment, the other was a child in a dark outfit, probably a boy, though Mr Potter could not be sure as he could not see the youngster's face as it was turned away at the time. Both figures were positioned about ten paces away from the farmer and looked solid in appearance.

Mr Potter went very cold as he watched the couple. Then, as he shone the torch at them, the woman turned to him and he could see she had bright pink eyes, which rooted him to the spot. Soon after, the couple turned and walked away from the farmer and a cow lying on the grass stood up and moved away as if acknowledging their presence. When they were out of sight, Mr Potter heard the gates of the adjacent graveyard open and shut.

At this, the farmer ran all the way back to the farmhouse to tell his wife who testified that he was still shaking for hours afterwards and that she had never seen him so scared in all her life.

The investigators were told by Mr Potter that a living relative of John Daniel had asked the couple to be shown the burial site of the young boy, and it seemed possible that this had triggered the appearance of the two ghosts.

Blandford

BLANDFORD ARMY CAMP

In 1952, three young soldiers were training in a battalion based at Blandford Camp.

Lying in their beds in their military hut one evening they were discussing their work for the following day while the rest of the platoon slept.

Suddenly one of them saw what could only be described as a 'thing' hovering outside the window. Seeing his expression the other two quickly leapt up to see what was there.

The object was of a classic ghostly appearance, with no facial features, and only a dark slit where there should have been a mouth, which kept opening and closing as if trying to talk, and stranger still they could hear the definite sound of someone or something scratching on the window-pane. After a while it moved to the fire escape and started banging on the double-doors, as if trying to get in. In fear, one of the men jammed his rifle through the handles so that the door would hold up against the banging and pushing.

As the rest of the platoon started to awaken due to all the noise the thing just disappeared. While two of the men hurriedly explained to the rest of the platoon what had occurred, the third soldier rushed outside but could find nothing to account for the sighting.

Summoned to the office the three men attempted to explain what had happened to the NCO who, inevitably, was very cynical about the whole affair until another soldier rushed in and explained that he had witnessed a similar thing. This man was a duty orderly and told how the 'thing' had entered the medical treatment room and started throwing things around the hut. Not surprisingly, the orderly flatly refused to return on his own.

The authorities seemed interested in the accounts, but nothing was ever mentioned about it again, although they continued to discuss it, off and on, for some time afterwards.

RIVER STOUR

A lady from Blandford, who wishes to remain anonymous, wrote the following letter:

"Perhaps you may like to hear about our 'ghost train'? One sunny afternoon in the mid-1970s, my husband and son (then a young boy) went fishing on the River Stour in Blandford. They settled on the riverbank in an area which was quiet and secluded, with no other people around.

After a while, both my son and his father, heard the sound of a steam locomotive in the distance and, as it grew louder, with the wheels pounding, they clearly heard the distinctive sound of its hooter. My son moved along the bank to his father and said: 'Did you hear the train, Dad?'

There was no train. In fact, the old line had been closed for several years, and all that remained was an old bridge, spanning the river, which had been partly dismantled.

My son, now a man in his thirties, still remembers it well, but as we were newcomers to Dorset at that time and unfamiliar with the area, we cannot pin-point the exact spot."

Bournemouth

John D. Tuffin, of Winton, Bournemouth, relates a whole host of spooky experiences.

"I moved to Bournemouth from London in 1979, leaving behind a house that had rather more than its fair share of supernatural occurrences! In 1980, I moved into my present address with my partner and my Jack Russell bitch, Tillie.

One of my first actions was to renovate the kitchen, which involved moving the old butler sink into a new position away from the window. On three occasions over the next four years, friends of ours told how they saw an elderly lady bending over the sink apparently washing clothes. What struck them as particularly strange was the fact that what they saw was taking place where the sink had originally been situated, prior to my moving it! They had no knowledge that I had moved it.

After Tillie died in 1990, she continued to make occasional visits, usually late at night, but sometimes in broad daylight. After we obtained a new dog, Garbo - also a Jack Russell bitch - we often saw both dogs sitting side by side. Believe me, it can be tiresome getting up in the night to go the toilet, to see a dog approaching the door to be let out, and when you go to open the door the dog disappears leaving the living one fast asleep in her bed!

When Garbo died, in 1999, she returned to us two nights later. We were sitting up in bed reading when we both felt the mattress go down as if Garbo had jumped on the bed, as she was in the habit of doing on cold nights. The duvet then lifted and my partner felt the familiar sensation of her pushing her head into our armpits for attention. On this occasion the attention she received was my partner having to reach for the asthma inhaler!

Since that night, neither dog has been seen or felt. We think that Garbo came to say goodbye, as she had died in our absence while having an operation at the vets.

In the same house, my mother was once woken up in the middle of the night by the figure of a man standing next to her bed (she was staying with us and sleeping in our bedroom). On her regular visits from then until her death a few weeks after Garbo's in 1999, she adamantly refused to sleep in that room. The figure she described seems to fit that of a man both my current partner and I have seen on numerous occasions looking around our garden. He is only ever seen out of the corner of one's eye and disappears soon after.

The final part of the tale concerns objects. On many occasions, objects such as keys or money disappear only to return some time later. These situations can, of course, be put down to forgetfulness, but two particular occasions stand out. One was when a pair of spectacles disappeared, then turned up two weeks later on the carpet in the dead centre of the lounge. We have been known to hoover, so they cannot have been there all the time!

The other occasion, and perhaps stranger still, was one Sunday evening while I was carving a joint in the kitchen. My partner's father called me into the garden to ask about a particular plant. I put the knife down on the worktop while I went to speak to him. Upon my return the knife had gone. A search of the whole area failed to find it, but after dinner when we returned to the kitchen to wash-up the knife was back in splendid isolation - in the middle of the worktop. It was a relief that at last my partner's sceptical father was convinced that the house held something strange.

Another such incident occurred the day my former partner and I moved into the flat in 1980. I left him in the house, while I went into the garden. When I wanted to come in again the door connecting the kitchen with a short passage leading to the back door had been locked against me. The key had been turned and removed from the lock. My partner had been in another room and had no knowledge of the incident, until my hammering on the door attracted his attention. I soon made it impossible for this action to be repeated - by removing the door!

It is also interesting to note that since I first wrote to you mentioning that neither of my dogs had been seen since the occasion of Garbo's 'farewell visit' Garbo was seen twice on the same day - the day I received your letter! My current partner saw her that morning sunbathing in the garden, adjacent to the spot where she is buried; and I saw her later, in one of her favourite positions, sitting on the sofa in the lounge staring out of the window at the passers-by."

Mr Tuffin and several members of his family and friends had odd experiences in two former houses in Bristol and London.

His then partner saw Mr Tuffin's maternal grandmother and one of his uncles. The latter was a tall man dressed in grey trousers, a collar-less shirt and braces. His partner was able to identify the relatives from old photographs that he had never been shown before. On the night of his partner's grandmother's death, Mr Tuffin was awoken by a huge dog sitting across his chest in bed. It wasn't until the next morning that they received news of the old lady's death.

After his father's death, he and several members of his family were awakened by the sounds of his father attempting to crawl up the stairs to the toilet, as he had done in the last few months before his drawn-out death from cancer. His mother was once awoken by the feeling of a hand touching her face, the way that his father was in the habit of doing during the night, reaching for a glass of water from the table by the bed.

Says Mr Tuffin: "In that same house I saw the ghosts of at least two different cats. It seems I am fated to be haunted by animal ghosts!"

In conclusion, he says: "My theory is, and always has been, that when we die we simply move into another dimension and continue in death to carry out the same actions we performed in life. Occasionally, some 'electrical charge' causes the two dimensions to cross over. In that sense we, presumably, are 'ghosts' to the other dimension!"

"It is only when writing these things down, that one realises how relatively ordinary the incidents are, which may go some way towards supporting my theory of different dimensions. On only two occasions have I ever been frightened by this kind of situation, and neither of these occasions was in either of the two houses I have been writing about."

"I feel that, generally speaking, what doesn't hurt us in life, will not do so in death."

Mrs Gill Wilson, also of Winton in Bournemouth, has always been sensitive in that she gets 'feelings' about people, events and buildings. Having sat in on a few psychic circles, she knows she possesses some psychic ability - and has seen ghosts from time to time.

When she worked at a children's activity camp in America, Mrs Wilson walked into one of the cabins which she shared with another member of staff and saw an old lady stood by one of the bunk-beds, who turned to her and half-smiled. Later describing her appearance to her colleague, the latter promptly told her she had described her late aunt. Mrs Wilson described the feeling she got when she saw this lady was that her aunt wanted her to know she was there and watching over her.

"A more recent episode," she explains, "was when I moved into my present flat in July 2002. Even before I had agreed to buy it, I kept getting this immensely strong feeling that just kept saying 'fire' over and over again. This was an understandable worry as the flat has only got one entrance and my son sleeps in the attic room, but the message was more than that and I knew I was being warned that there was something wrong."

"I mentioned it to the estate agent several times and considered a number of fire preventative measures, but it was very difficult to get any work done at the time, so I had to leave it and my children and I moved in anyway."

"I found it very difficult sleeping because I kept getting this very heavy feeling in my solar plexus which kept waking me up. A few months after we moved in I had to get the central heating sorted out which involved pulling the cooker away from the wall to gain access to the mains gas tap. We found that someone had done a very dangerous job with the wiring connected to the cooker and instead of finding a steel plate at the rear of the cooker some idiot had just put a piece of cardboard there instead. This cardboard backing was right next to the insulation material which had brown scald marks all over it and was obviously a serious fire risk."

"As a consequence the cooker was condemned and all the wiring connecting to it was switched off. After the initial shock the tension in my solar plexus disappeared and I fully understood what someone or something had been trying to tell me."

"Some years ago, while waiting for my brother who works at Bournemouth Town Hall, I was in conversation with the caretaker and

Bournemouth Town Hall.

asked him if the Town Hall was haunted. The reason being that I could feel a lot of sadness as I stood there."

"He told me that ghostly horses and carriages were still sometimes seen at the entrance, which used to be a lot grander. In days gone by the hall had been the scene of many fancy balls with people arriving in their grand carriages."

"The caretaker very kindly took me on a tour of the building, pointing out a few parts in particular and asking me if I felt or sensed anything about them. During the war the Town Hall was used as a hospital and a Ghurkha soldier committed suicide at the top of the building. A ghostly cat has also been seen in the building. And there was a lot of energy coming from a corner of an office where a man used to sit who has since died."

Mrs Wilson concludes, "I do love to visit old castles and stately homes, etc, and try to pick up the 'vibes' of the past. It's also comforting to know that people on the 'other side' look in on us sometimes to help and guide us."

Bovington Camp

CLOUDS HILL

It was May 1935. T.E. Lawrence, aka Lawrence of Arabia, sat astride the massive 1150cc Brough Superior motorcycle that was his pride.

Switching on, he kicked down the engine starter and the bike growled into life, giving a low throaty rumble. He headed out of Bovington Camp where he had been to send a telegram. He manoeuvred the cumbersome bike through the winding lanes heading back to Clouds Hill, his small brick-and-tile cottage, bearing the same name. Passing a bend he somehow lost control of the bike and came crashing to the ground, the bike scraping across the road and slamming into the opposite side.

He was just two hundred yards from home. Two delivery boys on their bicycles had seen everything, but stood there in disbelief, rooted to the spot. An army corporal, who had been walking through an adjacent field, had also seen the crash and came rushing over. Lawrence lay on the ground unconscious, his face covered in blood.

The events that followed are as mystifying as any relating to this well-known war hero and writer. Directly following the crash a black van was seen by the two boys speeding away from the scene. An army truck quickly arrived and Lawrence was transferred directly to the army hospital at Bovington Camp. Upon his arrival the war office applied a top security cordon, monitoring and controlling all communications concerning the accident.

During Lawrence's period in hospital, Clouds Hill was raided; books and private papers removed by person or persons unknown. In addition, army intelligence personnel spoke to the witnesses, especially the young boys who were interrogated for several hours, during which they were told not to mention the black van.

Six days after the crash, T.E. Lawrence died and an inquest was arranged two days later, during which no mention was made of the van and so no attempt was made to trace it. Accordingly, the inquest returned a verdict of 'accidental death' and the case was closed but not before the coroner described the outcome as 'an unsatisfactory situation'.

Clouds Hill, Bovington Camp.

Stranger still was the reason that Lawrence had set off to send his telegram. He had received a letter earlier that morning from Henry Williamson suggesting a meeting be arranged with a little-known German politician called Adolf Hitler. Lawrence had wired back suggesting that arrangements should be made for them to meet, but his sudden and untimely death at the age of forty-six put paid to these plans.

Mystery still surrounds the death of Lawrence whose ghost is reputed to haunt the house and the lanes between Bovington Camp and Clouds Hill.

One couple who were walking along the road where Lawrence was killed claimed they could hear the distinct sound of an old-fashioned motorcycle in the distance which gradually grew louder, so much so that they expected it to appear round the bend in front of them. Suddenly the sound stopped and all was deathly quiet. Accompanied by a local man, who had been walking close by, the couple went to the corner and searched for any sign of the bike, but there was no sign of it or the rider. The man told them he had heard the sound many times before and believed it be the sound of Lawrence's Brough motorcycle re-enacting his final journey.

Another more recent report involved a family in a camper van parked at the side of the same lane, when they too heard the sound of an approaching old-style motorcycle - but this actually ended with the sound of a crash! On investigation no bike, let alone an accident site, could be seen.

In May 1985, an exorcism was held every day for a week in a bid to lay the ghost to rest once and for all, as local people feared that the ghost might actually cause a real crash! It is questionable, however, whether the exorcism was a success, as other ghostly incidents have been logged since.

Over the years, that stretch of the road became the scene of many sightings of the phantom motorcycle - even though it remained an aural haunting and was never, as far as we know, actually seen by anyone.

Bovington Camp is located nine miles east of Dorchester. Clouds Hill is one mile north of Bovington, with Gallows Hill lying just beyond.

The area is one of real beauty and tranquillity and it is not difficult to see why Lawrence loved it so much. On his discharge from the air force he bought the cottage and intended to spend his retirement there.

Although the ghosts discussed up to now have merely been spooky sounds, there have been a handful of reported sightings of Lawrence himself, in his cottage and in the garden, dressed in full Arabian robes and headdress. A lady who was visiting the cottage recounted one such ghostly experience. The lady had wandered into the music room and was casually glancing around taking in the atmosphere when she had the distinct feeling of someone behind her. Turning round, she caught a glimpse of what she took to be a white scarf-type material passing the door. Could this have been the ghost of Lawrence briefly returning to his beloved cottage?

Lawrence associated with some of the most influential people of the day and was visited by the likes of George Bernard Shaw, E. M. Forster and Robert Graves. He was also invited to join the Astor Set - the social trendsetters at that time. Lawrence had even kept the company of Winston Churchill - and was actually due to meet him on the day of his death.

Lawrence described his cottage at Clouds Hill as his 'paradise on earth' and spent the evenings reading, writing and listening to Beethoven on his wind-up gramophone. It was here that he wrote his famous book 'Seven

Pillars of Wisdom', recounting his exploits during the Great War.

His former home has been described as a perfect reflection of the complex person that was T.E. Lawrence and the semi-monastic way of life that he chose to lead at the cottage. Visiting friends recalled how they would be offered picnic-style food washed down with either water or China tea - but never alcohol.

The tiny rooms are just as he left them with simple austere furniture, some of which he made himself. The crowded book room is lined from floor to ceiling with hundreds upon hundreds of books. Under the roof-space is his music room, which contains his wind-up gramophone with the huge brass horn curving out over his listening couch. All around lay the 78-RPM classical records he loved to play.

Clouds Hill is now in the ownership of The National Trust and can be visited on selected days of the week from April to the end of September.

Lawrence's death remains shrouded in mystery, with many people believing he was murdered because of the accusations he cast at the British government. Following the Great War, the government failed to honour the promises that Lawrence made to the Arab people in return for their help during the conflict, a situation he found untenable and which ultimately led him to openly criticise the government of the day.

In retaliation he had rejected the offered post of Viceroy of India, and instead accepted the rather lower position of leading aircraftsman with the Royal Air Force.

Maybe his final act of insubordination in wishing to meet Hitler was considered one risk too many. Whatever the situation, it would appear that the ghost of T.E. Lawrence does not want to rest in peace.

He is buried in a small grave at Moreton, where the inscription reads: 'the hour is coming when the dead shall hear the Son of God and they that hear shall live.'

GALLOWS HILL

About one mile away from Clouds Hill lays Gallows Hill which, like another stretch of Dorset highway, Eggardon Hill, has witnessed its fair share of vehicles experiencing mechanical problems. But is this phenomenon a coincidental engineering failure, or is there another explanation?

Mr Cliff Rogers, of Weymouth, writes:

"One late evening in the late 1960s, I was driving my Ford Zodiac, travelling westward, down a stretch of road between Waddock Cross and Gallows Hill, just north of Bovington Camp."

"Suddenly there was a puff of smoke which seemed to emerge from under the dashboard and all my lights, including the ignition, went out and I ground to a halt."

"I climbed out to investigate, lifted the bonnet, but found nothing. Back in the car, I turned the key in the ignition and to my surprise the lights (except the headlights) all came on. The car started okay, and I resumed my journey home. Next day it was found that the headlight fuse had blown.

Three weeks later, I was taking my parents to London, thus travelling eastward this time, still on the same stretch of road, when suddenly the engine cut out and the car ground to a halt. Up with the bonnet again, but nothing was obviously wrong. I returned to the car, which re-started, but suffered power loss, managing a top speed of about 35-40 miles per hour. We decided to continue our journey at least for a few miles. Lo and behold, after passing Gallows Hill, the car bucked up and we carried on to London without a hitch."

"I thought it was just a coincidence, until an article appeared in The Dorset Evening Echo, as it was called in those days, saying that other people had experienced similar problems on the same stretch of road."

"I believe at the time the MoD, which was based at Bovington Camp, denied that any of their equipment would cause a problem to road traffic. Could it have been some secret electronic equipment? Who knows?"

"Of course, the ghost stories surrounding Lawrence of Arabia, who was killed on his motorcycle near this spot, and the fact that his cottage was nearby, came to the fore. So I am afraid poor old Lawrence got the blame for the occurrences, at least as far as the local people were concerned."

"The occurrences were very infrequent and I know of none since. I have worked at Bovington for the last thirty years, since 1973, and apart from the fact that some locals say that they have heard his motorcycle, I have heard of no more motoring incidents."

❧

Gallows Hill, Bovington Camp.

Bridport

GIPSY LANE

Now in her Seventies, Mrs Marie Metu, of Weymouth, still vividly remembers when she witnessed the Gipsy Lane ghost one sunny day in September 1934.

"At the time, I lived with my family in South Street, Bridport. Myself, my sister and a friend with our baby brother in a pushchair, were knocking down conkers at Gipsy Lane, off Pymore Road. At that time, there were no houses there, just a few trees and a dirt track."

"Suddenly, a lady of about sixty years old appeared from nowhere. She wore an Edwardian dress, veiled hat, shoes, stockings, and carried an umbrella - all entirely grey - even her face was grey! The lady reached her arms out to us and smiled - a particularly sickly smile, I remember - but we were all so scared we just ran like hell!"

"My sister got hold of the pushchair with my brother in it, my friend grabbed her bike and we ran all the way to the Salvation Army Hall on Priory Lane, where our parents were attending a meeting. When we told them what had happened, my Dad said we had seen the Grey Lady, who had been seen by other local people before."

"My friend, who lived in a village nearby, and who often passed down Gipsy Lane, always took the long way round, twice as far, flatly refusing to return to that spot."

"I have since heard of other people seeing the Grey Lady and my sister knows someone who has personally witnessed her."

"The four of us still talk about it now, even though I was only seven years old at the time - nearly seventy years ago!"

THE BULL HOTEL

There is a theory that this inn, situated on East Street, was originally built on the site of an ancient graveyard, perhaps explaining why

The Bull Hotel, Bridport.

mediums claim that there are many spirits at work here. In fact, the field situated directly behind the building is called 'Mortarhay' - which directly translated means 'field of the dead'. Many psychic fairs have been held here as a result as it seems to be a centre for paranormal energy and activity.

In a military skirmish, during the Monmouth Rebellion, Colonel Venner and several of his soldiers shot two local men, Edward Coker and the oddly named Wadham Strangeways. They allegedly haunted the room until the window from which they were shot was eventually blocked up.

People have felt inexplicably uncomfortable in the function room which served as a hayloft above the stables when the Bull was a renowned coaching inn. And a disembodied child's voice has been heard in the ladies' lavatory on the first floor.

Bridport Arms Hotel.

THE BRIDPORT ARMS HOTEL

This 17th century thatched building, which was used during the making of the TV drama 'Harbour Lights', boasts various supernatural happenings including the mysterious sound of footsteps, the rattling of glasses, taps turning on and off - and a sinister presence in other parts of the hotel, which has alarmed visitors and residents alike. While filming a TV programme here, the appearance of a stain in the shape of a human hand inexplicably appeared on the ceiling!

BROOMHILL FARMHOUSE

Situated to the left of Bridport by-pass, this four hundred year-old building is haunted by a member of the Golding Family who owned the property for several generations. The appearance of a phantom, dressed in a cloak, was apparently witnessed by a group of holidaymakers as recently as 1997, suggesting that perhaps there is some truth in this dusty old legend after all.

THE ART GALLERY AND MUSEUM

Situated on South Street, this 16th century building is hard to miss with its prominent central porch jutting out onto the pavement. It began as The Old Castle Inn and has variously served as a bank and two clubs. In 1928, Captain Albert Percy Codd bought it and presented it to the local Borough Council who re-opened it as a museum.

Dramatic temperature changes have been the reported occurrences by a multitude of staff and visitors over the years, and an occasional glimpse of a former owner dressed in a yellow Edwardian smoking gown - still on display in the museum.

A museums officer, Jane Burrell, recalled one gentleman visitor who feared to enter the building because of a group of people who were congregating around the ground-floor fireplace. However, this confused Ms Burrell, as she had seen no one in that room - and the fireplace had been screened off, with no one allowed near it!

Brownsea Island, off Poole

Ms Angela Morris, of Bournemouth, writes:

"When I saw your letter in the paper appealing for people to write to you, it reminded me of an experience I had, in 1982, when I was fourteen years old."

"My boyfriend and I were at the far end of Brownsea Island in some woods. I was looking down at some brick foundations, but was astounded when I looked up again. I saw fire and people screaming and running towards the sea. There were horses and men - some riding - all running around in confusion. It was just like a video being played in front of me."

"I went very pale and clammy and my boyfriend told me that I was transfixed and could not move. He made me sit down and I eventually told him what I had seen."

"Later on, when we went back to get on the boat, we visited a gift shop which sold books, one of which detailed the history of the island describing a fire, but I cannot remember the details or why it happened. Perhaps you could let me know if you find out anything?"

❧

Corfe Castle

Corfe Castle has a long and rich history dating back to Saxon times and the many chapters in its existence have given rise to numerous accounts of ghosts and various hauntings.

The ghost of Edward the Martyr, who ascended to the throne after the death of King Edgar in 975 AD, reputedly haunts the castle. Edgar had been on his second marriage, his first wife having passed away. His second wife became Queen Elfrida and after a short while she gave birth to a son whom they named Ethelred. Queen Elfreda harboured a hope that some day her son Ethelred would become the next King of England. She even pleaded with the King that Ethelred should be next in line to the throne in favour of Edward, but the King was determined that his first son and rightful heir to the throne would be next in line.

With the passing of King Edgar in 975 AD, Edward became King and Elfrida began plotting his demise. Edward was a regular hunter on the land around Corfe Castle and one day as he returned from a day out hunting, he was met on the path leading to the castle by retainers of Elfrida. Edward was stabbed to death and his body thrown unceremoniously down a nearby well.

Local people used the well frequently and soon stories began to emerge about strange lights that had been seen near the well. Visitors to the well who had been ill soon found themselves cured and so the reputation of the well grew and spread.

Eventually, the authorities decided to excavate the well which revealed Edward's body. Once recovered the body was interred at the Church of St Mary's in Wareham. Edward was subsequently canonised by the Pope, and was thereafter referred to as Edward the Martyr.

Over the years and up to modern times, ghostly lights have been reported in the vicinity of the well and also around the castle ruins. A group of visitors who were visiting the area in 1991 claimed to have seen a bright orb floating six feet in the air near the gatehouse. When they tried to get a closer look it moved away from them, behind the ruined walls and out of sight. The group checked around the castle ruins but could see no more sign of the strange phenomena. They were sure that there were no other

Corfe Castle.

people in the area who could have been responsible. To further support these claims it must be stated that Corfe Castle is situated on a very obvious ley line and as these have always been associated with 'earth-lights', as they are known, they could have contributed to the many sightings of this strange phenomenon.

Corfe Castle has certainly had a colourful past. It was originally made of wood and then in the latter half of the 11th century it was rebuilt in stone under the instructions of William the Conqueror. For the next six hundred years it was used as a fortress by many English monarchs, then in 1572, the castle was sold to Sir John Bankes, Lord Chief Justice, as a second home.

The castle stayed in the ownership of the Bankes' until 1982, when Mrs H.J.R Bankes bequeathed it to The National Trust as part of the Kingston Lacey and Corfe Castle estate. As a trust site, the castle has become a well-visited tourist attraction that is open all year round (excluding Christmas Day and Boxing Day), between 10am and 4pm, seven days a week.

Over its long existence, the castle has endured many hardships, including battles, sieges and an authorised demolition by Parliament. During one period, whilst under the rule of King John, twenty-two noblemen were starved to death in its dungeons. Over the years people have claimed to have heard moaning noises in the area where the dungeons used to be.

A peasant girl, who betrayed the castle to Cromwell's troops during the English Civil War, was subsequently beheaded and her ghost haunts the path leading up to the castle and the area just outside the gatehouse. Numerous people have seen her headless form standing by the castle walls near the ruined gatehouse. One of the more recent sightings was in 1976 when she was seen hovering near the castle gates. On other occasions people have reported seeing the ghost wandering on the path leading up to the castle.

In 1973, with such a long history of hauntings, the castle became the subject of a television programme. 'The Burke Special Report' centred on retrieving sounds from the stones of the castle walls. The principle was to stimulate the stones electronically to release the ghostly sounds of the many people who have lived there throughout its five hundred year history. This idea came from the notion that stone acts as a natural 'tape recorder' picking up sounds from each era and storing them like a video recorder. The Burke Special Report was considered a serious documentary programme of the day and the researchers claimed to have heard fragments of speech that may have been up to five hundred years old.

King Edward II was held prisoner at the castle until he was removed to Berkeley, where he was murdered. Over the years, many people have heard strange conversations, spoken in a language of that era, which have been explained as being that of King Edward II complaining of his incarceration. These reports tend to support the claims made in the Burke Special Report, of released voices from history, although in the end the programme did not claim to be able to identify the voices.

Corfe Castle stands on a natural hill, on the principle route through the Purbeck Hills, and although only remnants of the castle remain the site provides some of the most spectacular views in England. The village of Corfe Castle can be approached from either Wareham to the north, or Swanage to the south, on the A351 road. A most beautiful village and castle, the area is well worth a visit, and it features all of the amenities one would expect from such a popular attraction.

What can be said for certain is that Corfe Castle is one of the most haunted sites in Dorset, it is open to the public all year round, maybe you could be the next person to experience one of its many apparitions.

❧

Creekmoor, near Poole

Miss Catherine White, of Poole, vividly remembers an odd event she experienced around 1979-1980:

“I was about four or five years old at the time and living with my family at a place called Millfield, at Creekmoor.”

“It was a warm summer’s day and I was playing with a friend of the same age. We decided to go and play in the local park that had a playground and a pond and was about five minutes walk from my home. Whilst there we saw some other children sneak off through the bushes and so decided to follow them.”

“Pushing our way through the bushes, we reached a gravel track, which I think is called Roberts Lane, leading up to a farmhouse. We had lost the others; I think they had ventured deeper into the wooded area that lays beyond. While I was looking around to see if I could see any sign of them I turned and looked up towards the farmhouse and saw something else.”

“It looked like a family. A man, a woman and two children, walking towards me. However, they did not look normal. They were transparent, green-skinned and dressed in what appeared to be rags. I know it sounds strange but I always compared their appearance to that of the green giant on tins of sweetcorn!

Anyway, I was absolutely petrified; it scared me greatly, so much so that I ran straight home in floods of tears and was consoled by my father. I still remember it vividly to this day.”

“I know it all sounds strange and that children do have vivid imaginations - but I never did have much of an imagination, and also I don’t know how a child of my age could have been aware of such things. I know that children can make things up, but I don’t think I could have made that up - and yet still be adamant about what I saw.”

“I would be very interested to hear of anyone else who has had an experience in the same place, although I know that new houses have now been built in that area.”

Dewlish, near Dorchester

BETSEY CAINE'S CORNER

Mr Edward Parsons, of Dewlish, writes:

"My family have lived in Dewlish since 1850. In the early nineteenth century, a local girl named Betsey Caine hanged herself in a farmhouse in the village and, although I don't know the reason, I assume it was because she may have become pregnant."

"My family bought the farmhouse soon after this event. My grandfather, Newbury Parsons (1858-1954), became the Church Warden, with whom I worked. In 1937 he was the sole Parish Council appointed by the D.C.C."

"He told me that the dead girl was buried under the wood at what has become known as 'Betsey Caine's Corner', which is situated on the road to Milborne St Andrew. It was the custom in those days to bury suicides at crossroads."

"Late one night, my grandfather was walking past the corner and saw Betsey sitting on the gate. He was not one to joke about such things."

"As we all drive cars today - and few locals live here anymore - one would not be walking the roads at night as was the custom many years ago."

Dorchester

ATHELHAMPTON HOUSE

Sometime during the summer months of 1969, Robert Cooke, MP for Bristol West and owner of Athelhampton House awoke in the early hours. Unaccustomed as he was to waking so early he looked around his bedroom with a feeling of unease. He was sleeping in the Grey Room at Athelhampton, his normal bedroom, when he suddenly saw his bedroom door open, then close, then open again. He sat watching the door, wondering who was going to come through it. He lay propped up on one arm and was alarmed when a bright light illuminated the doorway and the inner part of the bedroom. No sooner had the light arrived than it suddenly disappeared. The door remained ajar and the event was over.

This is one of the many ghostly occurrences that have happened to Mr Cooke and others over the years at Athelhampton House, surely one of the most haunted houses in the county of Dorset, if not the whole of England.

Athelhampton has a colourful history, not unlike many other houses whose history can be traced back some five hundred years. In 1483, Sir William Martyn received a licence from King Henry VII to enclose one hundred and sixty acres of land around Dorset and build a battlement house with towers. In 1485, with this approval in place, he built Athelhampton House, one of the finest examples of fifteenth century architecture, boasting some ten acres of landscaped gardens.

During the nineteenth century, Thomas Hardy's father was involved in the restoration of the Great Hall and the West Wing's roof, and it was during these works that Thomas Hardy first visited the building. He later went on to build his 'Athelhall' design on Athelhampton House and it was here during August 1914, whilst lunching with the owners, that news broke of the outbreak of the First World War. On a previous visit, Hardy had painted a watercolour of the South Front elevation showing the gatehouse that can still be seen today.

One of the strangest phantoms to haunt Athelhampton is that of an ape. The ape belonged to one of the Martyns in the sixteenth century and had freedom to wander around the house. At that time, one of the four

Athelhampton House, Dorchester.

daughters, having been involved in an unhappy love tryst, decided she no longer wanted to live and so ended it all in one of the secret chambers. As she set off down the secret stairwell leading to the chamber, the ape followed her but was trapped when the girl closed the chamber door behind her. The girl took her own life but in doing so she left the poor ape to starve to death on the stairwell. The girl's body was not found for quite some time by which time the ape had also long since perished.

Visitors to the house have enquired as to the strange scratching sounds that appear to come from behind some of the heavy wood panelling, only to be told that it is the ghost of the ape. One of the previous owners of Athelhampton, having heard the noise quite consistently over some period called out the services of a pest control company who informed him that there was no sign of any rodents or indeed any type of infestation. Is it just coincidence that in the Martyn's coat of arms, there is the image of an ape and that the same image can be found in the stained glass window in the Great Hall? Also, the Martyn's family motto is, 'He who looks at Martyn's ape, Martyn's ape will look at him.'

The house has remained pretty much unchanged since its inception, with each additional wing being built in the style of the original. The Great

Hall, with its complex wood roof and Flemish tapestry, are just as they were in 1485, when they were first installed. Therefore it is not surprising that such an authentic looking building should be the setting for TV programmes and films. In 1971 'Sleuth' was filmed here, starring Michael Caine and Laurence Olivier. Whilst making the film, the two actors were given quarters in the north wing as dressing rooms. It was here that Olivier said he felt as if someone was in the room with him even though he knew himself to be alone.

Over the years, Athelhampton has had a number of owners, at one point belonging to Sir Ralph Bankes, whose relations from the past had also owned Corfe Castle. Other owners include Sir Robert Long, 4th Earl, nephew of the Duke of Wellington, George Wood and Patrick Cooke, who is the present owner, and who has occupied the house since 1995. The house is open to the public and contains many magnificently furnished rooms and spectacular Grade I listed gardens, containing water features with ponds and fountains. The Great Court has pyramids and the Yew Trees are some thirty-five feet high. The formal gardens are balanced beautifully with woodland and riverside scenes as the River Piddle flows right around the boundary of the house.

Athelhampton House is open six days a week (Sun-Fri) from March to October and is then open on Sundays from November through to February. The house is easily found off the A35, five miles East of Dorchester at the Northbrook junction of the Puddletown bypass.

Probably the most famous ghost of Athelhampton House is that of the Grey Lady who has been seen on a number of occasions in the Tudor Room. A maid once claimed to have seen her sitting in a chair just when the house was closing up for the day. Believing the lady was a visitor the maid politely asked her to leave, at which point the lady stood up and glided through the wood panelling. On another occasion the housekeeper saw the lady stood in the Tudor Room; she described her as being dressed in old-fashioned clothing and wearing a gauze head-dress. The image faded once the housekeeper tried to talk to her.

As one would expect from a building of such grandeur, Athelhampton House was built atop a range of wine cellars, in keeping with the extravagant socialising and merriment that would have prevailed there. It is here, below the house, where the wine is stored, that another ghost dwells, and one that most visitors would rather not meet. A heavy wooden door whose locks originally came from Newgate prison bars the cellar, and many visitors have heard the hammering of a long dead cooper as he prepares the next barrel. One recent visitor said that she distinctly heard the tapping noise coming from just beyond the door and yet had been told that this particular door is rarely opened and, normally, nobody would ever be down there.

There is also the ghost of the hooded monk whom people have reported over the years. Historically, the monk is difficult to place and it is therefore believed that he was a rector, who wore a cassock and a 'shovel-hat' that gave him the appearance of a monk. It is understood that the rector was using Athelhampton as the setting for a book he was writing.

Other ghostly occupants of the house are the phantom duellists who appear in the Great Chamber. Every so often they play out their duel, until one appears to be wounded in the arm. There are no specific historical references for these spectral gunmen, but they have been seen on a number of occasions and heard on a number of others.

The various hauntings at Athelhampton reportedly continue to this day, so perhaps a visit to this wonderful old house would be a worthwhile excursion for any intrepid ghost-hunter!

Dorchester

WOLFETON HOUSE

Wolfeton House allegedly has three ghosts to its credit and by far the most bizarre is the phantom of Thomas Trenchard who owned the house in the sixteenth century. It is reported that on certain nights his ghost can be seen atop a spectral coach-and-four as he charges up the grand staircase! This is a strange report as in reality it is most unlikely that this event actually occurred and yet it is firmly embedded in the building's ghostlore, and remains the definitive haunting for which Wolfeton is now most renowned.

Wolfeton lies on the A37 between Dorchester and Yeovil and is indicated by a road sign denoting its status as an historic house. A Grade I listed building - a combination of both mediaeval and Elizabethan, Wolfeton is nestled in water meadows at the confluence of the rivers Cerne and Frome. Much embellished around 1550, it has magnificent carved oak panelling, splendid plaster ceilings, many grand fireplaces and a unique stone chair.

One of Wolfeton's other well-known ghosts is that of the Grey Lady whom many visitors to the house have seen over recent years. The Grey Lady is normally seen around Wolfeton's gatehouse. A woman from Dorchester reported seeing her stood by one of the circular towers which stand either side of the gatehouse. As she watched the ghost made a move as if to walk away but instead simply disappeared. This is typical of the type of reports regarding the Grey Lady.

The development undertaken by Thomas Trenchard represented the most prosperous period for Wolfeton House, and from that point forward the house sank into a gradual decline and was eventually abandoned, being ultimately sold to cousins of the Trenchards. By 1800, the chapter in the north wing was in ruins, and twenty-two years later other parts of the house were demolished. In 1862, the property was purchased by W.H.P. Weston who repaired the remaining buildings and in addition carried out a number of modifications. The present owner is a kinsman of the Trenchards and since 1973 has carried out a whole series of refurbishments.

The main house has now been restored to its original splendour, including

Wolfeton House, Dorchester.

the reproduction of detail in areas such as The Great Chamber, which is the setting for one of the other hauntings at Wolfeton. A young woman bringing an aura of great tragedy has been known to haunt this room. Thought to have been married to one of the previous owners she had, for reasons not known, taken her own life by slashing her throat. Although reports differ, the most common sighting is of this tragic young lady peering out from the window as if deep in thought. Similar to the Grey Lady, she simply fades away when approached.

Wolfeton House is approached via the Gatehouse, flanked by the two unmatching round towers. In one of these, now known as The Chapel, there can be found other interesting features of the property whose origins are unknown, including a series of wooden panels on which are the signs of the Zodiac. The Chapel and its immediate vicinity are also places where the Grey Lady has been seen.

Today, Wolfeton retains a substantial element of the original building designed by the Trenchard family and contains some excellent examples of seventeenth century paintings and furniture but, as you are now aware, Wolfeton also boasts a variety of phantoms to keep the attention of even the most demanding of visitors!

Presently the home of Captain and Mrs Thimbleby, the house is open to visitors between July and mid-September on Mondays, Wednesdays and Thursdays.

Eggardon Hill

The narrow lane which runs between Eggardon Hill and Powerstock village, has borne witness to a number of mysterious power failures. Like the similar 'haunting' of Gallows Hill, (see Bovington Camp), there are well-documented cases, involving cars and watches mysteriously stopping when they reach that part of the lane.

In addition, animals such as horses and dogs have been seemingly terrified of some unseen presence, and disembodied shouts and cries have been heard when there is no one around to account for them.

The spooky tradition of Eggardon's famous white deer is regarded as an ill-omen, which may or may not be related to this phenomenon, though some believe an untapped power source from the Iron Age hill-top fort may be somehow to blame for these ghostly events colliding with today's drivers and pedestrians who travel along this lonely route.

It may do well for Dorset residents to check the small-print in their motor insurance policies. It just may be the case that accidents and breakdowns due to spooks and spectres are one of the few exemptions for a successful claim.

Holt, near Wimborne

Mrs K. Snell, of Poole, writes:

"Some years ago between 1986-1988, my husband and I were visiting friends who had bought an old cottage at Holt, near Wimborne. The cottage is situated on God's Blessing Lane, where there is a triangle of grass called God's Blessing Green. The owners of the cottage were told that, in centuries past, the troops were blessed here before journeying to Corfe Castle.

Our friends had partly converted their new home into tea-rooms, during which they had discovered a very old partition wall. We had all spent a pleasant evening never once referring to the cottage or its history. When it came time to leave, I went through to the middle room which is part of the teashop to collect our coats.

As I opened the door, I froze in amazement. Standing in the corner, next to a latched door that led to a narrow staircase, were three figures. One was a woman wearing a long heavy dress and an apron, with something like a piece of cloth on her head and holding a tray. The other two were what I took to be soldiers. I assumed by the way they were attired that one of the men was of a higher rank, possibly an officer, as he wore a more elaborate uniform and wore what I took to be a sword on his belt. It seemed that I stood there observing for quite some time - but suddenly I was aware the group were gone.

I rushed back to the next room, but when I told my husband and our friends what had happened, they just did not believe me!

The image has remained so strongly with me that it still sends a shiver down my spine even now. It was a wonderful experience!"

Lyme Regis

BETTISCOMBE MANOR

Bettiscombe Manor is often referred to as 'the house of the screaming skull' and is one of a number of houses containing skulls with apparent supernatural powers, the most infamous one being Burton Agnes Hall on Humberside.

The manor has been in the Pinney family for hundreds of years and it is a member of this family that the legend of the skull and the ghostly happenings at the house are connected.

In 1685, following a period of civil disruption, Azariah Pinney and his brother were brought before Judge Jeffreys, charged with supporting the Duke of Monmouth. The judge found them guilty. Azariah was banished to the West Indies, whereas his brother faced the hangman's noose.

During his forced exile, Azariah managed to become a successful businessman and was eventually allowed to return to England and Bettiscombe Manor. The story suggests that Azariah also brought back a trusted Negro servant, whose only wish was that his body be returned to his homeland at the time of his death.

Eventually the slave died and he was buried in a local churchyard, although another version of events suggests that the Negro slave was murdered.

Following the slave's burial, terrifying screams and moans could be heard emanating from the grave and the windows and doors of the manor would swing open and shut of their own accord. The screams and poltergeist disruption continued for some time. One report even suggested that Bettiscombe Manor vibrated and shook down to its very foundations.

Eventually the slave's body was exhumed and for a while the ghostly activity ceased. Unfortunately, during the process of removing the corpse, the skull became detached from the body, but was kept at the manor and all remained quiet and calm again.

Over the years, the Manor was passed along the Pinney line, and one of the new owners took a dislike to having the gruesome skull in the house and threw it into an adjacent pond. Not long after this occurred, the

Manor was once again filled with terrifying screams, with doors and windows being forced open and shut. This time, however, the sound was not just confined to the Manor; workers in a nearby field also reported the deathly wailing.

Having been told of the ghostly legend, the owner of the skull had no option but to wade into the pond and retrieve the skull. Again, as soon as the skull was returned to its rightful place in the Manor, the mayhem stopped and all went back to normal. On other noted occasions, the skull has always reacted violently when it is removed from the house.

It is now believed to be kept in an old box, stored in the attic at Bettiscombe Manor, although other reports suggest it is hanging from an old beam in the roof.

The legend of the skull's origin may now be in question. It was recently carbon-dated, and the results suggest that the skull is some two thousand years old, and thought to have come from Pilsdon Pen, an Iron Age fort not far from the Manor.

Another story tells how the skull was buried at a depth of ten feet, in an attempt to cease the supernatural activity - but it somehow managed to

Bettiscombe Manor, Lyme Regis.

work its way back up through the soil to the surface. Once found, the terrified individual immediately returned the skull to the house, knowing that this was the only way to pacify the ageing relic.

Although others have suggested Azariah Pinney brought the skull back as a memento, it is not known why the skull should exert such powers. One popular theory is that the skull protects the Manor from ghosts - although this would appear to be a contradiction in terms given the skull's own effect on the Manor!

Bettiscombe Manor can be found just off the B3164, although it now forms part of a private residence and is no longer open to the public. Visitors should attend only with the approval of the present owners.

It is not known if the removal of the skull has been tested in recent years. A further twist to the tale suggests that whoever removes the skull may suffer a horrible fate within a year.

On balance, it may not be worth the risk!

THE ROYAL LION HOTEL

The Royal Lion Hotel stands next door to the former site of public executions; there are a multitude of ghostly chills wafting through this building. In 1973, landlords Alan and Susan Jones experienced a white shape, which passed through them. Mrs Jones said it felt like 'a damp mist going right through you, turning you to jelly!'

Others have heard footsteps approaching them accompanied by a 'cold, chilly sensation and doors slamming and banging throughout the building'.

Psychical researcher and author of 'The Haunted Pub Guide', Guy Lyon Playfair has experienced such 'cold spots' himself. He points out that they feel much more like 'a drifting mass of air' or 'a cloud of clammy air molecules' rather than a phantom wind, though he concedes it is hardly surprising why so many witnesses feel that this cold-mass effect is linked to ghosts and the supernatural.

LYTCHETT MATRAVERS

One of the farmhouses situated near a plantation of fir trees, on the road near the village of Huntick, is reputed to be haunted by the ghost of a man who follows its residents through the plantation and stands at their doorways peering in before disappearing.

The wooded area of Lytchett Matravers is also thought to be the haunt of a ghostly coach-and-four, though some local historians consider that this ghostly manifestation had been a ploy used by smugglers to keep superstitious people at bay, as the road running through the wood was one of the most notorious smuggling routes in the county.

Melbury Osmond

REST & WELCOME INN

The only 'ghostly' phenomenon reported here, though many, many times, was the bolting of the door, which resulted in customers attempting unsuccessfully to get in to the place!

The landlady at the time thinks that she may have caused the 'ghost' to appear - by telling her husband 'I wish the customers would all go home so that we could have the place to ourselves'; then she may have rid the pub of the 'ghost' by saying to it: 'if you don't stop bolting the door, we will have to leave, because the customers will not come in to buy our drinks.' The suspected ghost has not returned since.

Rest and Welcome Inn, Melbury Osmond.

North Allington

THE BOOT INN

Although the exact date for the inn's construction is a little vague, it is certainly very old. The first recorded landlord for the hostelry was Mary Braddick in 1758. Two phantom figures have been seen sitting at the left-hand side of the bar, one dressed in a khaki military uniform, the other in older style civilian dress.

An accident occurred here in the 1870s, when one of the customers was fatally injured by a customer's shotgun that went off accidentally. A forty-five year old customer suffered a full blast to the head and died later that day. His ghost, dressed in mid-19th century attire, haunts the position along the bar where the accident occurred.

If you ever get taken ill in the bar and are offered sanctuary on the floor above - politely refuse. A grey lady appears to sick occupants on the first floor. According to legend, she is the landlady of the King's Arms who was murdered by a cavalier, though why she should haunt here and not the latter pub, situated some way down the road, is unclear.

Poole

POOLE HIGH STREET

In the mid-Sixties, a shop attracted attention from the local media when staff and customers encountered the antics of a ghost that they nicknamed 'Jenkins'.

The branch manager often saw objects in the shop moving around of their own accord which caused some of the customers to flee in fright. The building had been planned for demolition to make way for a large-scale development project in Poole High Street, and it was rumoured that the resident spook was not at all happy with this arrangement!

Two years previously reports of the haunting had been received and now another resurgence of paranormal activity was witnessed again. One customer saw four bottles of after-shave float off the shelf and drop to the floor, while her husband saw a travelling bag unhook itself from the shelf, hang in mid-air for a moment, before also dropping to the floor!

BYNGLEY HOUSE

This four hundred year-old merchant's house has, for some poor visitors, created a very frightening feeling of being suffocated. Some people have emerged from one particular upstairs bedroom feeling faint, almost as if someone had tried to smother them. Some years ago the remains of a mummified cat were found nailed to the floor joints of the house and this was discovered to be one of the ways in which residents attempted to keep evil spirits at bay!

THE CROWN HOTEL

In 1989, landlords Malcolm and Pat Miller experienced a number of odd incidents in the five weeks since they had taken over the Crown Hotel, which is situated on Market Street.

The Crown Hotel, Poole.

Lights had flickered on and off in the cellars, an icy chill had greeted people on entering some of the rooms. Visitors had heard the sounds of people moving around on the upper floors when there was no-one there, and the sound of piano-playing drifted in from the barn. Tools and nails had been found thrown around the barn. An unidentified woman had appeared in a window on the top floor and the sound of horses' hooves had been heard in the courtyard - both day and night. And perhaps more frightening than all was the sound of a body being dragged across the floor.

Although this seventeenth century pub has always had a spooky reputation, it was not until the mid-1960s, when much of the modern phenomena were reported. A previous landlord, Mr Alan Brown, started to convert and reconstruct some of the outbuildings and, as students of the paranormal will no doubt be aware, this activity is seemingly the cause of many paranormal happenings throughout the world.

Changing the structure, internal or external, of a property, tends to spark off ghostly happenings. The reason for this is anyone's guess, but is it possible that some long-forgotten routine of a building's former occupants is somehow trapped in the original structure of a building, then begins to play back whenever that structure is physically disturbed?

During the restoration work, an old room, with no doors or windows, was discovered in the attic. It does not show on any known plans and no purpose for the room can be found.

A well-known paranormal researcher, Dr Peter Hilton-Rowe, examined ancient records and the account of how a former landlord had imprisoned his two deformed children in the hayloft of the barn - and eventually murdered them. In fact, one of the phenomenon regularly experienced is the sound of terrified children screaming throughout the building.

One account came from a man called Eric Drayman, who was at the hotel with two friends, Paul Eeles and Malcolm Squire, whilst it was being renovated in 1966. They were standing in the courtyard when they all heard a single note being played on the piano in the upper room of the old hayloft. This room in particular was being renovated so it could be used for dancing.

"When we heard the note," said Malcolm, "Paul, who lived at the hotel, said it was a ghost. I thought he was pulling my leg."

The young men investigated but the room was empty - yet the note was still being struck. Suddenly, everything on top of the piano showered onto the floor."

At this point, they ran outside and watched what they described as a 'fluorescent mist' move down the staircase, across the courtyard and disappear through the hotel entrance.

A visiting Australian, Mr D. Browne, who was staying at the hotel, said he thought the men's experience had been a trick of the imagination and set about proving it. He bolted the door of the old room and watched it unbolt and open by itself.

He told the Poole and Dorset Herald newspaper "it was the most eerie feeling I have ever had in my life."

THE GUILDHALL (SCAPLAN'S COURT)

Once a town house but now preserved as a museum, the Guildhall was the scene of a gruesome double murder. In 1598, the mistress of the house, Alice Greene and her maid, Agnes Beard were attacked and brutally murdered by four robbers, intent on stealing money bequeathed to Alice on the death of her husband William Greene.

The four robbers heard of the £200 inheritance and thereby plotted to steal the money. Richard Parmiter, Roberte Hill and Godwin Spencer, led by the then mayor John Beryman, (the latter only lived next door) burst into the house to find the maid sat on the stairs eating her supper.

They hit her on the head once, a full blow with a hatchet which killed her instantly, and then went in search of the widow. She was killed with a dagger through the heart and a barking dog suffered a similar fate. Then the four made off with the loot. Although there is no record of what happened to three of the robbers, Roberte Hill took the blame for the murders and was hanged for the deaths the very next year.

Scaplan's Museum, Poole.

An attendant of the Scaplan's Court Museum, Mrs Joan Patch, said she remained convinced that the ghost of Agnes haunted the building. A woman with an apron emerges from the buttery, crosses the courtyard and goes upstairs, witnessed by several of the attendants at the time.

A dog has also been heard to bark, which of course could relate to the time of the murders, and Mrs Patch had seen a man with a white beard, wearing a cloak and standing in the room, three times over a two-year period.

She said of the man 'he's rather lovely', and, although she can sense him and other events in the house, it remains a pleasant home with a friendly, warm atmosphere - irrespective of its grisly history.

SKINNER STREET UNITED REFORMED CHURCH

A sub-editor of the Poole & Dorset Herald newspaper reported how he had visited Skinner Street United Reformed church and had seen the old-fashioned high box pews and brass lamps. On a subsequent visit, the interior of the church looked completely different, with these items no longer on show. Enquiring of the vicar, he was flabbergasted when informed that those particular pews and lamps had been removed from the church - more than one hundred years before!

Sandford Orcas, near Sherborne

SANDFORD ORCAS MANOR

Following the destruction of Borley Rectory (Essex) by fire in 1939, Sandford Orcas ascended to the grand title of the 'most haunted house in Britain'. Boasting upward of twelve ghostly spectres, it certainly lives up to its chilling reputation.

Built in 1540, around the time of Edward the Confessor, Sandford Orcas reputedly stands on the site of an ancient Saxon dwelling. Of Tudor design and built of golden Hamhill stone, the building is virtually unaltered since its original construction. The dull stone walls, tall mullioned windows and the peering gargoyles that stare down from each of the building's gables serve to compound the eeriness of the house even further.

Sandford Orcas, known more commonly as the Manor, can be found in the village of the same name, near to the town of Sherborne. It is

Sandford Orcas Manor.

approached on the B3148 and then simply follow the signs that will direct you along the leafy lanes to Sandford Orcas. This beautiful village or the Manor house will not disappoint you, should you dare to visit. Sandford Orcas Manor can be found next to the village church and is approached via the gatehouse, beyond which you will find yourself looking at the most haunted house in the land.

In the possession of the Medleycott family since 1736, the house has been leased out to many families over the years. The house was occupied by Colonel Francis Claridge and his family from 1965-1979, who regarded it as being haunted in the extreme and even claimed that as many as fourteen ghosts were at large in its Tudor rooms.

Over the years there have been reports of a Lady in Green, a Lady in Red, a phantom monk, a yokel nobleman, an Elizabethan lady, and even a seven-foot high ghost. The ghost of the nobleman was said to be that of Sir Hubert Medleycott who had hanged himself in the gatehouse.

One of the strangest tales relates to a room at the back of the house, entered via a large and heavy door equipped with an observation hole, in which a young man, deemed to be insane, was locked up during the waxing of the moon. At other times, this young man was apparently quite normal, enough to be allowed to wander unrestrained through the village. The young man had been training at a naval college, and was expecting to commence a promising naval career. However, whilst there, he killed a fellow cadet. Having been declared insane, he was sent back to Sandford Orcas and it was in the room at the back of the Manor house, in his late twenties, that he died. He was subsequently buried in the grounds of the house. The story persists that his screams can still be heard coming from the room.

In more recent times, a young man visiting Sandford Orcas with his girlfriend, had been granted permission to enter the room, more to impress his girlfriend than anything else. However, no sooner had he entered the room, than he rushed back out in a state of severe shock. Composing himself, he explained that on entering the room, a man had rushed at him and tried to kill him.

One of the most unpleasant ghosts at Sandford Orcas is that of the seven-foot tall villain, known as the 'stinking man', who was thought to have been an 18th century footman at the manor. His curious nickname came

Sandford Orcas Manor.

about as a result of the odour of decaying flesh that he always left behind him. This unfortunate soul has been seen wandering from the gatehouse to the staff quarters where he would knock on each of the bedroom doors. When this fellow was alive he was said to have been a rapist and that he had seduced every female member of staff employed at the manor. It was initially reported that his ghostly form only appeared to virgins and that it was always accompanied by the sound of a body being dragged along the corridor. A visiting psychic investigation team allegedly managed to photograph the ghost with the aid of infra-red equipment, and the result clearly shows the form of a tall man in Georgian dress.

The gateway has been the scene of much drama over the years. One of the tenant farmers who lived at the manor hanged himself from a pulley in the archway of the gatehouse. The farmer's ghostly form, wearing a white milking smock, has been seen walking across the front lawn on many occasions. This phantom was also photographed, his ghostly white form being quite clear in the print. However, the photographer caught the image quite by accident and it wasn't until the photographs were developed that the ghostly presence was noticed. It is almost certain that this was the ghost of James Davidge, the tenant farmer who took over the tenancy in 1748. A figure matching this description has been seen several times over the years, peering in through the kitchen window.

The notoriety of Sandford Orcas has seen it the subject of various investigations including one filmed for television by the BBC. Its reputation grew further when a member of the crew who was staying at the house claimed to have seen the ghost of an old-fashioned farmer dressed in a farmer's smock and hat. The television exposure brought in more reports from former members of staff and visitors, all of whom claimed to have had ghostly experiences.

Following the BBC's visit, a group from the Paraphysical Laboratory, at Downton, visited Sandford Orcas and subsequently submitted a report of their findings to the Journal of Paraphysics. In the report they claimed to have evidence to support the history of ghost sightings; indeed, they claim to have verifiable evidence of five specific hauntings outside of those previously claimed by the Claridge family.

In the sixteenth century, the Knoyle family owned Sandford Orcas. This was at the time of the Stuarts. One of the Knoyle sons has been photographed at the window of the Great Hall, wearing his Stuart hat. The identification was made from an old painting that still hangs in the house today. On another occasion the ghost of Edward Knoyle was seen by a visitor and identified from an old sketch.

Over the years many visitors have stayed at Sandford Orcas and some have had terrifying experiences. A lady from Taunton claims that she saw a phantom swaying at the foot of her bed whilst sleeping in the nursery wing. She says he was dressed in evening dress and his form was clearly silhouetted against the window. 'His face was evil-looking,' she said. 'He stood there for quite a while, then disappeared.'

Mr A. Daniell, who lived at the house in 1900 when he was ten, described how a 'very nice old lady' used to come and visit him on many occasions, whilst he was sleeping in the solar, which served as his bedroom. According to Colonel Claridge, two ladies also reported seeing the ghost when they used the solar as their sleeping quarters.

Colonel Claridge himself claims to have seen many of the ghosts that inhabit the house. One evening, when the last of the visitors had left the house, Colonel Claridge was staring out across the main lawn when he saw a woman dressed like a gypsy come through the gate and onto the lawn. As the house was now closed to visitors, Colonel Claridge was somewhat annoyed at the intrusion, especially as the lady had not sought permission. In an effort to establish what this lady wanted Colonel Claridge walked towards the woman and she simply melted away.

Another phantom that apparently appeared to the Claridges, known as 'The Moor', appeared in their bedroom for seven nights running. Each time the Colonel would awake to find the ghost staring down at the four-poster bed, before fading away. When the seven days were up, the phantom did not appear again for twelve months. Keen to establish the identity of the phantom, and armed with the anniversary dates of the sightings, Colonel Claridge was able to use old records to narrow down his search. He quickly came across the record of a murder that had taken place at Sandford Orcas. The phantom that had looked down on him as he slept was that of a Moorish servant who had killed his master while he slept in the bed, by pressing down a length of wire against his throat.

The four-poster bed featured again when Claridge awoke to find the ghost of a priest leaning over the bed as he lay there, his wife asleep next to him. The priest looked to be holding out a length of his cloak as if preparing to smother him. This particular apparition was banished when the Colonel took to hanging a crucifix in the bedroom. When asked what significance he thought this sighting had, the Colonel ventured that he thought the house may have been used for black magic rituals in the past and that this could explain the high level of supernatural activity. He believed that the phantom priest could have been involved in black mass and to lend further strength to this argument the Colonel pointed to the scene shown in one of Sandford Orcas' many stained glass windows, in which a goat features, as if about to be sacrificed. To most Christians, this scene would have been quite

Sandford Orcas Church.

unacceptable at the time.

Another ghostly vision backed up by hard physical evidence involves the appearance of a lady from the Georgian period, dressed in a red, ornate hand-painted dress. Subsequent to the sighting a similar hand-painted dress was found hidden in a chest in the priest hole.

In addition to the many spectral men and women, Sandford Orcas also boasts its very own ghost dog, a fox terrier, once belonging to a woman who had given birth to a son at the Manor. This ghostly pet can only be seen on the anniversary of its death.

Tapping sounds that could not be easily explained or traced have also plagued the manor. Soon after moving into Sandford Orcas, the Claridges began hearing strange tapping sounds coming from the staff quarter. Colonel Claridge's daughter was so taken with the mystery that she decided she would spend a night there to see if there was any truth in the story. After sleeping for a while she was violently woken from her slumber having been hurled to the floor by some supernatural force. She had the feeling of invisible fingers wrapped around her throat and after a struggle was able to flee from the room. So shocked and scared by the experience was she that she vowed never to enter the building after nightfall.

The period of time over which the sightings have been occurring at Sandford Orcas make this a difficult haunting to dismiss. Many people from all walks of life and from different generations and indeed centuries have lain claim to seeing phantoms and ghosts in various parts of the manor. For twenty years from 1966 Sandford Orcas Manor must have been the most prolific haunting in the country and will therefore, for the purposes of this book, maintain its title of 'the most haunted house in Britain'.

For those readers with an iron nerve and a thirst for exploring the unknown, Sandford Orcas Manor is still sat next to the church in Sandford Orcas village, waiting to display its ghosts to anyone who dares to call.

❧

Shaftesbury Abbey

Shaftesbury Abbey was once one of the main abbeys in England and during its peak was home to as many as three hundred and fifty people. The Abbey was founded by King Alfred the Great as a Benedictine community in 888AD. This area of the country was busier at this time and the Abbey became a focal point of the community providing financial prosperity for the next six hundred years.

There are many mysteries and stories surrounding the Abbey and of course these would not be complete without mention of the ghosts who inhabit the ruins. The ruins have been subject to a number of archaeological digs and excavations over the years and in 1931 a lead casket was unearthed containing the skeletal remains of a young Anglo-Saxon boy. The identity of the boy is a continuing point of controversy. In 1971, a group of people seeking some excitement visited the ruins after a night of revelry and were met by a young boy darting in and out of the shadows. It was after midnight and the visiting adults were surprised to see such a young lad out and about. Mysteriously, whenever the group thought they were getting nearer to the boy, he would appear at the other end of the site, behind them. Eventually all went silent and the boy apparently vanished into thin air. Could this have been the ghost of the young Anglo-Saxon boy?

The Abbey was also held in great regard by the then royal head of Denmark, King Canute. It is reported that he had requested that upon death his heart should be taken to the Abbey and buried within the grounds.

The corpse of King Edward the Martyr, murdered at Corfe Castle, was finally laid to rest at the Abbey and today his final resting place is marked for visitors to see.

The wife and daughter of Robert the Bruce were detained at the Abbey for two years during the conflict with Scotland and were finally released after the Battle of Bannockburn.

The Abbey also played host to Catherine of Aragon who stayed over whilst making her way to London to marry Prince Arthur.

One of the legends of the Abbey is that there is a haul of buried treasure

Shaftesbury Abbey.

somewhere amongst the ruins. The story goes that one of the monks buried the treasure to safeguard the Abbey's wealth during a troubled period, but unfortunately the monk died of a heart attack before he could pass on the secret location to anyone else. Over the years excavations have unearthed a number of historical artefacts but the treasure remains stubbornly elusive.

The most well known and best documented of the ghosts who haunt the Abbey is that of a hooded monk. The monk has been seen walking along the edge of one of the Abbeys crumbling walls, passing through a space where it is known a door previously existed. It is not known for sure if it is the same monk who buried the treasure but the local superstition has it that the monk is either guarding the treasure or will not rest until he can pass on the details of the treasure's whereabouts.

One of the strangest details of the haunting is that those who have reported seeing the ghostly monk have reported that he appears to be walking on his knees. It is thought however that the monk is walking on the ground level as it would have been at that time and that since then the ground level has risen. This particular feature would be consistent with other reports of hauntings on Roman roads and the like, where people have seen whole legions of Roman armies all apparently cut off at the knees.

The Abbey's gradual decline into the bare ruins that are the remnants today came upon the order of King Henry VIII, who in 1539 gave orders for the Abbey to be dissolved. The Abbey was then stripped of its treasures and the inhabitants of the area raided the abbey for its stone.

Over the next few hundred years the Abbey fell into total ruin and in 1985 was passed to the stewardship of the Shaftesbury Abbey & Museum Trust Company. The Abbey is now open daily from April to October and can be found just off the High Street in Shaftesbury between Park Walk and Bimport.

There are further excavations to be carried out this year and we shall have to wait and see if the treasure is finally found or if the phantom monk decides to lend a helpful or mis-guiding hand.

THE GROSVENOR HOTEL

This is probably one of Trusthouse Forte's most ancient inns, and is reputed to be haunted by a Monk and a Lady in Grey. The former has been blamed for the disappearance of several beer bottles in the cellar, while the ghostly lady has been seen dashing around the building in an agitated state. Interestingly, there are many old tunnels, which zigzag their way under the historic market town of Shaftesbury - and one theory is that the monk, at least, is connected to a story relating to this underground labyrinth.

Sherborne

SHERBORNE CASTLE

Sherborne Castle can be found a little to the south of Sherborne, just off the A30. Among the remnants of the original castle are the walls and gatehouse.

The Castle has had a most colourful history and is better known today as the historical abode of Sir Walter Raleigh. In 1592, Elizabeth I leased the old castle to Raleigh, who initially enjoyed the splendour of his surroundings. However, as time passed, Raleigh decided that the cost of repairing the castle was too much for him to sustain and so he decided to build a new property in the grounds of the castle. This was thereafter referred to as The Lodge and construction was commenced in 1594.

During the course of the next decade Raleigh gradually fell from grace until he was imprisoned in the Tower of London and finally executed in 1618. Following his death the property was passed to Sir John Digby, who himself lost favour with the monarchy through his inability to arrange a suitable Royal marriage with the Spanish monarchy.

Digby retired in disgrace, returning to Sherborne where he devoted much of his time to adding new wings to the building, giving it the castle-like appearance it has today. The Digby family has been in continuous occupation since that time.

The main haunting at the Castle is said to occur on St Michael's Eve, when the spectre of Sir Walter Raleigh is reputed to haunt the old garden where, having done his rounds, the ghost gently fades away, near an old oak tree which is named after him.

It is thought that the haunting is connected to a curse that was placed on the property as a means of ensuring the Castle never fell into lay hands. Following the Conquest, the site was given to Osmund, who later became the Bishop of Sarum. A dispute followed as to the ownership of the land when the Earl of Salisbury claimed he had sole rights. It was initially thought that the rightful heir may have to be decided through a duel to the death, but the Bishop managed to retain ownership and the episode passed without the spilling of blood. However, following this challenge, the curse was placed to ensure that the church always retained control

Sherborne Castle.

over the property. The curse seemed to have worked well as all subsequent non-clergy owners have all met with premature deaths, including Raleigh and the Earl of Somerset both of whom were executed.

However, the curse appears to have faltered somewhere along the line. Now in the ownership of Baron Digby, he and subsequent generations have all resided there without trauma.

Raleigh appears to be doomed to wander the gardens for eternity. During the summer months of 1983, when some work was being undertaken in the castle grounds, one workman, having completed his chores for the day put his tools in the back of his van, then returned for a brief wander around the Castle gardens. That day the Castle's gardens had seen its last visitor leave by 6pm. The time was now approaching 7.30pm and so the workman was not expecting to see anyone. He was therefore surprised to see a gentleman dressed in 'old-style clothing' wander across one of the lawns and then out of view behind some trees. His interest aroused, the workman quickly ran across the lawn to see who the man was but, as is so often the case in hauntings, there was no sign of him anywhere.

Could this have been Sir Walter Raleigh? If so, the tradition of his ghost only being evident on St Michael's Eve would appear to be inaccurate. Whoever it was we shall never know, but what we do know is that it adds further to the mounting evidence of ghostly activity at Sherborne Castle.

Sixpenny Handley

The following is an article passed onto the authors by psychical researcher Robert Snow, who is featured in the chapter 'A Chilling Task'. *It concerns an intriguing experience related by his Grandfather:*

THE BRONZE AGE HORSEMAN

By Dr Richard Chaloner Cobbe Clay

"In 1924, I was in charge of the excavations carried out by 'The Society of Antiquaries' on the Late Bronze Age Urn field at Pokesdown near Bournemouth. Every afternoon, I drove down to the site and returned at dusk."

"One evening, I was motoring home along the straight road which cuts the open downland between Cranborne and Sixpenny Handley. I had reached the spot between the small clumps of beech trees on the east Squirrels Corner and pinewood on the west, where the road dips before rising to cross the Roman road from Badbury Rings to Old Sarum. I saw, away to my right, a horseman travelling on the downland towards Sixpenny Handley; that is to say, he was going in the same direction as I was going. Suddenly, he turned his horse's head, and galloped as if to reach the road ahead of me and cut me off. I thought he was just a stable-lad from the racing stables two miles further back along the road."

"I was so interested that I changed gear to slow down so that we should meet, and that I should be able to see who the man was. However, before I had drawn level with him, he turned his horse again to the north and galloped along parallel to the road and about fifty yards from it."

"I could see he was no ordinary horseman, for he had bare legs and wore a long, loose coat. His horse had a long mane and tail, but I could see neither bridle nor stirrup. His face was turned towards me, but I was unable to see his features. He seemed to be threatening me with some implement, which he waved above his head in his right hand."

"I now realised he was a prehistoric man, and did my best to identify the weapon so that I could date him. After travelling alongside my car for about two hundred yards, the rider and horse suddenly vanished. I noted the spot and found next day, when I drove along the road in bright daylight, that the spot coincided with a low, round barrow close to the east side of the road. I had never noticed it before."

"Many times afterwards, at all hours of the day, when I was weary, when I was alert, I tried to see my horseman again. I tried to find some bush or other object which my tired brain might have transformed into a horseman, but with no success."

"I made some enquiries in the district and, after a few months, Mr Young, the well-known iron craftsman of Ebbesborne Wake, told me that he had asked many of his friends at Sixpenny Handley if anyone had ever seen a ghost on the downs between the village and Cranborne, and that at last an old shepherd, George Raymond of Gussage, and formerly of Alvediston, had asked "Do you mean the man on the horse that comes out of the opening in the wood called Squirrels Corner?"

"A year or two later a friend of mine, Mr Alexander Keiller, a well-known archaeologist, wrote to me as follows: 'your horseman has turned up again. Two girls, daughters of Harry Foyle, of Oakey Farm, Handley, cycling from Handley to Cranborne one night to a dance, complained to the police that a man on a horse had followed them over the downs and had frightened them."

"Mrs Young, wife of Mr James Young, told me recently that she was at the family tea party when her husband mentioned to those seated at table what Mr Keiller had said in his letter to me. The daughters of Harry Foyle, being cousins, were at the party, and said that they were the girls mentioned in the letter, but had not mentioned it before for fear of ridicule."

"Captain B.H. Cunnington, the curator of Devizes Museum, had told me that his grandfather and Colt Hoare had opened the barrow and found in it the bones of a man and a horse."

"Mrs Young and her son recently told me that the account which old shepherd Raymond gave to Mr James Young was as follows. Shepherd Raymond used to feed his sheep on Handley Downs every day. He took his dinner with him in a red handkerchief. When he had finished his dinner, he always smoked his pipe. One day, after he had finished his dinner, sitting on a bank near Squirrels Corner, he saw, as he was filling his pipe, a man on horseback come out of the green lane between the trees on his right. He did not recognise the horseman. Finding to his dismay that he had no matches in his pocket, he hesitated, then got up and walked towards the horseman, who had turned his horse towards him, intending to ask him for a light. Just as he approached the horseman, both the horse and man vanished."

Copyright Robert M. Snow.

❧

Tarrant Gunville

EASTBURY PARK

Built by Lord Melcombe in 1718, the huge house at Eastbury Park was ranked third in size to Castle Howard and Blenheim Palace. Although construction began in that year, it was not completed until 1753, and even then there was still additional construction work continuing for a further ten years.

Acquired by Lord Temple in 1763, half of the house was subsequently pulled down to save the cost of its upkeep. By 1775 only the North Wing remained standing, though even then this had to be let out as tenements to labourers employed on a nearby estate.

Lord Temple had a steward named William Doggett who spent much of his time relieving his employer of funds meant for building costs. If that was not enough he also flogged much of the building materials intended for the rebuilding of Eastbury Park House.

When Temple discovered his steward's treachery, he ordered the latter to

Eastbury Park, Tarrant Gunville.

repay a huge insurmountable sum and, when he couldn't, ordered that Doggett be arrested. On the eve of his arrest Doggett made his way to a particular panelled room in the house and shot himself.

Traditionally, suicides were buried at crossroads, for superstitious locals believed that the dead would rise again as vampires - and they determined that Doggett would not have this option, with the ensuing possibility he would return to wreak revenge on them. However, unusually for such a case, the deceased steward was finally and riskily laid to rest at Tarrant Gunville Church.

On certain nights Doggett's ghost, complete with a yellow silk ribbon tied around his breeches, can be seen alighting from a phantom coach, complete with headless horseman. Here the fraudulent employee heads straight to the room where he shot himself. Witnesses say then that all is quiet for a moment, before hearing the awful sound of one final gunshot - for this is where the ghostly re-enactment ends.

In 1450 Tarrant Gunville Church was re-built, which included the exhumation of a number of bodies, including that of William Doggett. Intriguingly, historical records state that Doggett's body was evident with a yellow silk ribbon tied around his legs. His face, still rosy and far from decomposed, is a sure sign that Doggett's suicide granted him eternal life as one of the undead.

Thorncombe

FORDE ABBEY

Forde Abbey can be found four miles to the south-east of Chard on the Dorset/Somerset border, concealed amongst a network of winding country lanes, the perfect setting for a traditional English haunting. Therefore it is somewhat surprising to learn that there is only one ghost likely to be seen at this most historic building.

Founded by Cistercian monks over eight hundred years ago, Forde Abbey became one of the richest and most learned monasteries in the country. In the sixteenth century, Thomas Chard spent much of his time restoring the Abbey, enhancing it with a splendid gothic facade. After the Dissolution in 1539, when the Abbey was surrendered to King Henry VIII, the building remained empty for one hundred years and suffered much deterioration, including the destruction of the church.

In 1649, the Abbey was bought by Sir Edmund Prideaux, a wealthy lawyer, parliamentarian and attorney general for Oliver Cromwell, who stylishly transformed the Abbey, incorporating much of Chard's earlier work, creating the beautiful building we see today. The Abbey then went through a succession of owners, before falling into the hands of the Roper family at the beginning of the twentieth century.

Throughout this period, the house has been the scene of a number of ghostly happenings. The most common description is that of a figure

Forde Abbey, Thorncombe.

dressed in a monk's shawl tied at the waist, who can be seen moving slowly along the monks' walk - part of the cloisters.

Judging by the descriptions provided by those who have witnessed this rarely-seen phantom, it is thought most likely to be that of Thomas Chard. It is known that Chard, the last Abbot in residence, had a great regard for Forde Abbey, with its large and peaceful gardens and so it would not be surprising to find that he wished to remain here even after his death.

The Roper family continue to inhabit the house and have kept the property true to its original architecture and decoration. Consequently, its appearance has remained virtually unchanged for the past three hundred years. Much of the interior dates back to the ownership of Prideaux, with an abundance of oak panelling and intricate plaster mouldings.

The grandest room in the house must surely be the salon, once adorned with the Abbey's most important pieces of art, but now with a series of well-preserved hangings based on Raphael's original sketches for the Sistine Chapel.

One of Forde Abbey's most spectacular rooms, The Grand Hall, is another haunt of the phantom monk. Chard, if that is the identity of the ghost, is often seen stood by the large dining table, gazing out of the windows over the gardens he so loved to wander through.

Although the apparition has not been seen so frequently, visitors can take their chances, as Forde Abbey is open to the public from Tuesday to Thursday, from April to the end of October. The Abbey gardens are open daily throughout the year from 10am to 4.30pm and the Abbey House from 1pm to 4.30pm.

Forde Abbey, Thorncombe.

Tyneham, near Weymouth

Christopher Grist took a photograph outside the window of a derelict cottage in the 'lost' village of Tyneham.

It wasn't until sometime after it had been developed that his partner asked if he had superimposed an image on the photo with his computer - which he hadn't.

He said there seemed to be a ghostly image on the photo and although he was sceptical of ghosts, Christopher, of Bournemouth, said 'but there's definitely something there'. He said it looked like the image of a man appearing between the trees in the background.

Some people think they can see the shape - but others can't see anything at all.

The photo he took a few seconds before does not reveal the mystery shape and he has returned to the village since to see if the foliage could have caused an optical illusion.

"It's a bit unnerving," he told the Bournemouth Daily Echo on Tuesday 25th February 2003. "It looks like a man in a greatcoat with a flat cap on. Could it be a soldier?"

Others who have seen the photo also say that the figure looks like a soldier but that he is wearing a helmet rather than a flat cap.

The village is 'lost' because it was evacuated in December 1943 and, for reasons unknown, the villagers never returned. Christopher appealed for anyone with spooky experiences at Tyneham to come forward and share their tales.

Wareham

In 1991 Mr Adrian Brown, a security supervisor, was driving his van towards a roundabout near Wareham when he noticed a company van - exactly like his own - with the same distinct company logo on its side - driving towards him. As it passed him he saw that the driver was his exact double!

He is adamant that the driver was not a lookalike - it was himself - and that the van was identical, even though there were only two vans for this company, one of which he was driving while the other was currently off the road.

Interviewed in 1996, five years after the event, by a journalist for the Daily Mail newspaper, he said he was still adamant that he had seen his own doppelganger. Although it no longer bothered him he did have bad dreams at the time and was fearful for what the future might bring and what it could all possibly mean.

At the time of writing Mr Brown is fine and has had no further experience of this kind. If he has a double he has presumably left town.

West Allington

THE PLYMOUTH INN

Built in the eighteenth century, the Plymouth Inn has one of the strangest ghosts on record - a small furry monkey! Although it has only been reportedly seen once - by the young daughter of a previous landlady - some customers have felt it brush past their feet as they sit in the bar. Thinking it is the pub cat they have been surprised to see the resident tabby sat quietly at the other end of the bar!

Weymouth

Mrs Jacqueline Whayman-Pover writes:

"One night, when I was seventeen years old, I had gone to bed around 10pm as usual and as soon as my head touched the pillow I was fast asleep.

I have always been a light sleeper - though a sound sleeper - so I was a little surprised to suddenly awaken while it was still dark. As I couldn't get back to sleep, I just lay there thinking of recent things which had happened. I had lost a dear relative a couple of months earlier, so I may have been thinking of her.

However, as I lay there, a sort of mist appeared in the middle of the room, which formed into a human figure - about five feet in height. I think it was a woman, because there was an outline of what I took to be a long skirt, but I didn't recognise her.

I tried to look away but couldn't for some reason; the figure did not move, except to hold out her arms. I believe that whoever it was wanted help, but I was shaking and it was difficult to know what to do for the best. I remember starting to pray and managed to look away briefly, and when I looked back the figure had transformed back into the misty shape and then it was gone.

I lay there for the rest of the night, wide-awake, trying to come to terms with what I had seen, and who it could have been. My Dad had told me that before our family moved to our present house, a woman used to live there who read tea leaves - could it have been her? Or perhaps my relative whom I had previously lost. I just don't know...."

Wimborne

THE BARLEY MOW, BROOM HILL

On one occasion, the notorious 'Broom Hill Blob' of the Barley Mow public house was seen by six people in December 1978, described by one of them as 'a sort of shapeless haze over the fireplace,' which was visible for about half a minute before vanishing.

Landlord David Parker and his wife had both seen something on other occasions, though it is difficult to describe this vague form or the reason behind the haunting.

Barley Mow Public House, Wimborne.

Appendix I

'A CHILLING TASK'

The Ghost Club of Great Britain has been investigating hauntings since it was formed in 1862 and past members have included the novelists Charles Dickens, Dennis Wheatley and Sir Arthur Conan Doyle. While membership was initially limited to invitation, the Club has since thrown its doors open to anyone with an interest in the subject of ghost investigation.

In this section we meet two members of the illustrious Ghost Club - both with Dorset connections.

Robert Snow has been Secretary of the Ghost Club for the last six years. Born in Salisbury, Wiltshire, he now lives in the village of Iwerne Courtney, near Blandford.

He first became interested in the paranormal through his grandfather, the noted archaeologist Dr Clay, whose sighting of the Horseman of Sixpenny Handley (reproduced in this book) was one of several unexplained experiences throughout the latter's life.

One of Robert's most fascinating experiences occurred during an investigation at Pengersnick Castle, near Praa Sands, Penzance, Cornwall, on the evening of 4th and 5th April 1997.

At the time there had been no recently reported activity at the Castle. Although there are many legends attached to the Castle they are, in most cases, just legends with no documented eyewitness accounts. Also, many are probably fabrications dreamt up by smugglers who wanted to keep superstitious locals away from their nefarious activities by concocting tales of white ladies, phantom monks and headless horsemen.

Neither the owner nor anyone else had previously described the ghost, which the team subsequently experienced at the Castle, and no records exist regarding this particular phenomenon.

However, the ten investigators - eight men and two women - arranged to spend a night in what is known as 'the haunted bedroom'. Each member of the team positioned themselves so that they could see as much of the room as possible.

One of the group, a Mrs Don, was sat in a chair by the window. Just after midnight the lights were switched off and although dark, the room was partly illuminated by the moonlight shining in through the window. The group sat in silence for about four minutes, until Robert and some of the others saw something. A white, misty shape seemed to be appearing by Mrs Don's right shoulder, as she sat in the chair by the window. It seemed quite dense and roughly the shape of a person.

The figure seemed to be swaying from side to side as if shifting its weight from one foot to the other. This motion continued for about fifteen minutes before finally fading away, at which point the team switched on the light.

After excited discussions between the team members, the light was switched off once again and after a few minutes, a figure - possibly the same one - began to materialise. It was white in colour and stood to the left-hand side of the bed, as the team faced the foot of it. It seemed a mixture of being fairly faint to very bright - but it was clearly visible at all times. It seemed to be female, wearing a straight dress and around 5'6" in height. "It's face was of a greenish-greyish colour - not lifelike at all," Robert tells me. "And I still remember the way that it kept shifting in and out of focus. It was very strange."

At this point, the figure started walking towards Robert. As three of the members present had not seen the figure or witnessed any other paranormal activity that night, Robert called out to them that the figure was heading in his direction. As he repeated the words, the figure stopped and returned to its position. "It did not turn around," said Robert. "It just seemed to walk backwards."

It was at this point that someone suggested one of the team should walk towards it. "And guess who volunteered?" quips Robert. He started walking towards the figure, but halted within five or six feet of it. He described the feeling as 'extremely cold'. "It was just like walking into an industrial cold-store," he said.

He is adamant that the figure looked straight at him and turned to him as he had approached it, thus acknowledging his presence and therefore displaying at least some degree of intelligence.

Some of the team, including Robert, also thought they could make out another figure lying on the bed, though less distinct than the other. After a few minutes both figures faded away and when they did not return the light was switched back on.

Robert Snow is quite certain that this was not an optical illusion caused by the moonlight. Seven out of the ten investigators present saw the image and, although there were minor discrepancies between each report, the descriptions tallied. All the witnesses wrote up their accounts individually and the next morning they compared notes. It was obvious they had been watching the same thing.

But the question remains: why did three out of the ten investigators not see anything, when the others clearly did? Robert is unsure as to the reason. "It could be that they were sitting in a position where they could not physically view the phenomena, though admittedly there wasn't much in the way of furniture which could have obscured their vision. It could be that seven out of the ten people present were susceptible to the phenomena, for whatever reason, and the other three weren't. But the jury is still out on that one."

Although he has been to Pengersnick Castle both before and since that night Robert Snow has not experienced anything further at that location.

* * * * *

W. T. G. (Tom) Perrott, FIWO, was born in Bridport, Dorset, but then moved to London with his family at the age of four where he still resides. However, he still retains a great affection for the county of his birth, and has even subscribed to the Bridport News to stay in touch with local news and events!

Born into a family background which he terms Non-Conformist and Liberal, he cultivated 'an early attitude of detached independence and a slightly anti-establishment feeling'. During the war he served in the Reconnaissance Corps before transferring to the War Office for Prisoner of War Intelligence. Tom maintains that his interrogation of prisoners served as useful experience in later years when he went on to interview witnesses of psychical phenomena. With an early interest in legends and folklore and local history in general he made a particular study of Dorset history and served for several years as Secretary for The Society of Dorset Men.

He has published many articles, book reviews and short stories and is co-author with Rodney Legg and Mary Collier of 'Ghosts of Dorset, Devon and Somerset' (1977), has contributed chapters to several volumes such as 'Strange Dorset Stories' and has written forewords for a number of books on the subject of the paranormal - including this one! It thus seemed a natural progression to investigate accounts of modern ghost lore.

He has been a lecturer and investigator for the SPR (Society for Psychical Research) for many years and during his countless interviews in newspapers and magazines and on radio and TV, journalists often ask him the question: 'what equipment would you take on a ghost investigation?' to which Tom invariably replies 'a pen, a notebook and a sympathetic ear'. Tom maintains that in many supposed cases of hauntings it is the witness who needs investigating, rather than the house where they live.

The SPR once sent Tom to a shop in East London, which sold leather goods, as they had experienced a spate of poltergeist-like activity. Odd things were reported, like the toilet chain constantly being tied into knots, and other seemingly trivial occurrences, common among reported poltergeist disturbances. Knowing that many poltergeist cases seem to be centred around a young person - usually female - Tom asked the manager if there were any employed in the shop and was told that a young lady worked in the office.

As a retired Personnel Officer for a large bakery company, Tom is very much a 'people' person and is confident he can size them up fairly quickly. "However," he says, "having never met the lady in question, I could not give an opinion as to the reality of the phenomena. Whether it was genuine poltergeist activity centred on her - or if she was merely physically responsible for the incidents, I would not like to say, but I suggested that she be transferred to another branch. The manager took my advice and the phenomena ceased immediately."

One particular incident, which Tom remembers, occurred while Tom was staying overnight at The New Inn, in Gloucester. He had been on a business trip in the town when a huge downpour of rain had flooded many of the town's streets, so he decided to book in for the night with plans to continue his journey to Wales the following morning.

During the night he awoke to hear the sound of a woman crying in the next room, which was apparently empty. As he was pressed for time, Tom did not ask the owner as to the identity of the lady in question, but on returning home he consulted a book about local hauntings and found that The New Inn was traditionally haunted by a Woman in White, and that Lady Jane Grey had stopped at the Inn on her way to London, where she was to be crowned Queen. Although Tom is not entirely certain if he experienced a genuine haunting this episode has remained etched firmly in his mind, and is one account he often recalls when delivering lectures on the subject of the paranormal, as he does throughout the country.

A particularly intriguing experience occurred in the company of former President of the Ghost Club and prolific author Peter Underwood, and recounted in the latter's book: 'The Ghost Hunters'. Visiting a reputedly haunted property, Spencer Grove, in Stoke Newington, Tom, Peter, the Reverend John Robbins and one of the occupants went on a tour of the house. The property had a history of ghost sightings and other associated phenomena over the previous five years, including the sound of footsteps, knockings, unexplained fires, a groaning noise and misty smoke-like apparitions.

The electricity in the house had been completely cut-off so the four walked in complete darkness, their route illuminated only by torches. On one of the upper floors the occupant showed them the tall hanging wardrobe in one of the bedrooms from which the White Lady was said to emerge.

As the group left the room Peter Underwood thought it a good idea to 'tempt the entity' and made two loud knocks on the wardrobe shelf, before closing the door and descending the stairs. Alarmingly, the sound of two, clear, distinct knocks suddenly rapped back at the group from the totally empty room! After a brief investigation no reason could be found for the ghostly echo.

Tom Perrott has taken part in many radio phone-in programmes on the subject of ghosts and the paranormal and remains consistently impressed with the sincerity of the majority of people who recount their experiences to him. People who join phone-in discussions often do so as a last resort because they are experiencing things they can neither explain nor control;

desperate for assistance, they simply do not know where to go for help.

While he is sceptical of much phenomena reported in the media as 'terrifying' or 'horrifying' hauntings and the events sensationally dramatised in movies, Tom says that the true hauntings usually concern ghosts which seem to re-enact some routine - seemingly almost trivial - perhaps reflecting the activities or tasks which those people performed many years ago in their day-to-day lives.

Says Tom: "Cases which remain questionable are those where a person has visited a house, knowing the details of the haunting beforehand and then comes away saying they have experienced something - even if they didn't really see, hear or sense anything."

"The really intriguing cases, however, are different people who visit a property, with no knowledge of a haunting - their visits completely independent of each other - and it turns out that they report identical experiences. These are the convincing ones," he says.

Tom concludes: "It is so easy to accept every haunting as genuine or, alternatively, to dismiss every haunting out of hand."

"In fact, each case must be judged on its own merit."

Appendix II

'SHADOWS AT MY SIDE'

Retired electrical engineer, Royston Breeze, has been an active medium for fifty years.

He realised he was psychic from an early age when living with his family in Bow, London. One of his earliest experiences was at the funeral of an elderly neighbour, Mr Frew.

"Watching the procession as it moved up the street, I could clearly see the dead man, wearing his best black suit and peaked flat cap, walking ahead of the coffin. I told my maternal grandmother, 'Mum', but she told me what I had seen was Mr Frew's twin brother, who was walking behind the coffin with the rest of the family, but I was adamant that it was the dead man himself, clearly walking ahead of it. He did not look at me, but walked slowly, staring straight ahead. Some spirits actually enjoy their own funerals!"

"On another occasion, whilst serving at the Royal Air Force station, Linton-Upon-Ouse (North Yorkshire), I had the strongest sense that the King had passed away, so I hurriedly entered the crowded office of my NCO, Flight Sergeant 'Chiefie' Hicks, and told him what I had felt. The unexpected response was a shocked silence.

The Squadron's Engineering Officer, Flight/Lt Ford said: "Corporal, where did you get this information from? I demand a complete answer and the name of your source."

I felt I could not supply an adequate reply, and so fell silent.

Fl/Lt Ford barked: "Put this man on a charge, Flight Sergeant!"

Later that day, the sad news of the death of the much-loved King George became public knowledge. Good old 'Chiefie' conveniently 'forgot' the incident because of the pressure of the Squadron's funeral arrangements. To this day I continue to say my piece, without the fear of applied authority."

The only negative experience Roy Breeze has ever experienced as a psychic was the criticism initially levelled at him from his own family, as a youngster.

"They thought I was either mad or bad - discussing things I saw happening around me, when nobody else could - and I received a heavy dose of castor oil as a reward!"

And here is a message to grown-ups, particularly parents. If a child says they can see things or people which you can't, do not be so quick to scold them for 'making things up'.

"If children really experience these psychic images, and are then told that these images are not real - or that it is wrong to discuss them - then this could hamper a child well into adulthood."

Roy stressed the work of Dr Arthur Guidham, who claimed that many psychiatric patients, conditioned by society into believing they were 'seeing things', may well have been psychic - thus receiving biased diagnoses from sceptical doctors, then promptly pumped full of drugs and locked away from society.

"Do you ever have sudden flashes of inspiration which come out of the blue? This is often from spirits who want to influence people to do greater things. They can no longer directly influence the Earth themselves, so they attempt to do it through influencing the living. Writers influence writers, doctors influence doctors, artists influence artists and so on. Whatever that person's vocation in life - they will continue to follow that interest in death."

"Of course," says Roy. "There is a downside to everything. Have you ever had a sudden bad thought - perhaps a thought of violence against someone, for no apparent reason? Take time to wonder where that thought came from before acting on it. Spirits can influence us in this way, too. There are possibly people serving prison terms for murder or other violent crimes who did not know what they were doing or why they were doing it - and possibly still cannot come to terms with why they committed such a crime."

"However," adds Roy. "The moral stance of each of us determines the nature of our thoughts. The contact between creation, human or non-human, is by thought. There is not so much the consideration of what is Good or Bad - but what YOU personally accept or reject, as your attitude to living."

Roy has worked in development circles for psychics - using a number of different methods. Psychometry is one such method. "You hold an object which belongs - or has belonged - to a person and you get a sort of reading on the state of that person and their whereabouts. And no matter what the object is, or for how long it has been in the possession of someone, it retains a 'filament' of that individual's personality."

Mediums work in different ways, such as trance, mental or physical. Some feel a need to sit with their eyes tight shut in deep concentration, whilst others can achieve spirit communication no matter where they are or what they are doing at the time.

Some mediums and paranormal investigators say that there are different types of ghosts: spirits, apparitions, visitations, etc, but Roy prefers to avoid such precise classifications.

"People - in body or spirit - are individual; unique. Everyone is different; just as every birth and every death is different."

* * * * *

Olga Bamforth has been actively involved as a spiritualist medium since 1995. The first time she realised she was psychic was as a young girl, living in Halifax, West Yorkshire - coincidentally, less than a mile from the home of co-author Andy Owens!

As a child she had an invisible playmate. Says Olga: "As it turned out, it was the spirit of my twin sister who had died when she was just three days old."

She later moved with her family to St Ives, in Cornwall, before moving to Ferndown, Bournemouth, with her partner, who is a psychic artist.

Olga worked on her medium skills in a development circle for fifteen years and now works for clients who require private sittings. Occasionally she gets called out to the home of a person who is experiencing phenomena they cannot explain or comprehend, and she regularly tours the Spiritualist Church circuit in Southern England.

"I was devastated when my mother died and desperately wanted to make contact with her spirit."

She had also been a spiritualist - which she used to call The Old Faith - and has been in touch with Olga since her death.

"I have made contact with both my parents - but my father has come through to me much more clearly."

"When I am holding a private sitting and a spirit comes through to me, the connection between the spirit and the relative or friend, is often rather trivial - like a nickname for example, or a line from a song."

"One mention of that "connection" and the sitter recognises it straight away. To anyone else, it would be meaningless, but to the person who comes for the sitting, it is proof to them that the spirit of their loved one is here beside them and wanting to communicate with them."

Olga maintains that the sitters, either in a development circle or a private situation, must keep an open mind.

"A closed or sceptical mind could break the circle and make communication impossible."

One particular experience which Olga remembers is how she had a spirit come through to her, to pass on a message to a person in a church congregation. The recipient was amazed that the spirit could make such a contact - for her friend had only just died that very morning!

Some spirits who contact her remain earthbound because they feel they have unfinished business, or perhaps do not understand the reason why they passed on and want to continue to be around their family and friends. These may include what is known as poltergeist phenomena. "Poltergeist activity is the work of naughty spirits," says Olga. "They are merely trying to attract the attention of the living," she explains.

"Be aware of different sensations - particularly those which change suddenly. Obviously, some of them can be explained away in natural terms, but when the temperature changes dramatically, from cold to warm or vice versa, or if you are overcome with a feeling of sadness, anger or joy for no apparent reason, this is often because a spirit has come close. This presence often comes across as a spine-tingling sensation. You can feel the energy coming from them."

Olga and her partner are set to leave these shores for warmer climes, where they will continue their spiritualist work in Tenerife, but Olga feels that she is not merely teaching *others* about the afterlife; she remains adamant that she will continue to be a student of the subject herself.

Says Olga: "No-one knows everything. The more knowledge I gain about the spirit world, the more it makes me realise just how little I really do know!"

"There is always something new to learn."

About the Authors

Chris Ellis is married with three children. He has shared an interest in mysteries and the paranormal with Andy Owens since they were both teenagers, and they have co-written one other book together on the subject of true crime, *The Killer Catchers.* Chris Ellis lives with his family in a small village near York, north Yorkshire.

Andy Owens has written articles for many magazines including *Fortean Times*, *Prediction*, *True Crime Monthly* and *Writer's News* and is the author of several books including two about Yorkshire's ghost stories. He is a member of paranormal group ASSAP (The Association for the Scientific Study of Anomalous Phenomena) and lives in Halifax, West Yorkshire.

Notes

Notes

Notes

Notes